THE HAPPY VALLEY SKETCHES OF KASHMIR AND THE KASHMIRIS

From a photograph by Mr. H. Simpson. — Stanford's Geog.l Estabt.

THE CITY OF SRINAGAR, VIEW FROM THE GREAT MOSQUE

THE HAPPY VALLEY
SKETCHES OF KASHMIR AND THE KASHMIRIS

W. WAKEFIELD

"Who has not heard of the Vale of Cashmere,
With its roses, the brightest that earth ever gave,
Its temples, and grottos, and fountains as clear
As the love-lighted eyes that hang over their wave?"
Lalla Rookh.

WITH MAP AND ILLUSTRATIONS

GYAN

Published by

GYAN

Gyan Publishing House
5, Ansari Road
Daryaganj, New Delhi-110002
Phone: 011-47034999, 9811692060
E-mail: books@gyanbooks.com

Distribution Network
gyanbooks.com
India, USA, Canada, UK, Australia, France

ISBN : 978-81-212-3471-9 (PB)
First Published, London, 1879

2nd Impression 2020

Printed at: Gyan Press, Delhi.

The Happy Valley Sketches of Kashmir and the Kashmiris
Author: W. Wakefield

THE HAPPY VALLEY:

SKETCHES

OF

Kashmir & the Kashmiris.

BY

W. WAKEFIELD, M.D.,

AUTHOR OF

"OUR LIFE AND TRAVELS IN INDIA."

"Who has not heard of the Vale of Cashmere,
With its roses, the brightest that earth ever gave,
Its temples, and grottos, and fountains as clear
As the love-lighted eyes that hang over their wave?"

Lalla Rookh.

WITH MAP AND ILLUSTRATIONS.

LONDON:
SAMPSON LOW, MARSTON, SEARLE, & RIVINGTON,
CROWN BUILDINGS, FLEET STREET.

1879.

To

THE DEAR COMPANION

OF MY WANDERINGS, BOTH IN INDIA AND KASHMIR,

This Volume

IS AFFECTIONATELY DEDICATED

BY HER HUSBAND,

THE AUTHOR.

PREFACE.

DURING my sojourn in India, in the service of Her Majesty, as a medical officer to the Forces, I had the opportunity of constantly meeting and talking with numerous friends and travellers, who had visited Kashmir. From their observations, joined to what I gathered from the somewhat scanty literature treating of that country, I was fairly well acquainted with the subject of these pages before I had the good fortune to visit the Happy Valley for myself, and verify the ideas I had formed from hearsay and books. This event took place in the summer of 1875, and although our visit was short, we travelled over great part of the Valley, saw the objects of interest most worthy of attention, and examined closely into the manners and customs of the inhabitants.

From what we saw, and from that which I had previously gathered, the following pages have been written, and I venture to lay them before my readers as being descriptive of Kashmir and its inhabitants. I do not do so with the object of providing any intending tourist with a guide-book, for the descriptions of roads and distances are not minute enough to fulfil that purpose, which, indeed, is already provided for in the reliable *Hand-Book* of Dr. Ince, to which I was myself much indebted when in the country, and have been equally so during the progress of the present work. My design has rather been to present to those who have never visited the country, and, perhaps, will never have that pleasure, a short and general description of the routes to Srinagar; the history, manners and customs of the inhabitants of this beautiful province; and a sketch of the various places and objects of interest to be met with in the space of a short tour.

12, CAMPDEN HOUSE ROAD, KENSINGTON,
June 5th, 1879.

CONTENTS.

CHAPTER I.

CHAPTER II.

CHAPTER IX.

CHAPTER X.

CHAPTER XI.

CHAPTER XII.

THE HAPPY VALLEY.

CHAPTER I.

Introduction—The Punjab—The Vale of Kashmir—Its Beauty and Celebrity—Its Antiquity—Origin of the Name—Wilson's Opinion—Vigne's Opinion—Geographical Definition of Kashmir—The Surrounding Mountains—Gap in the Ring of Mountains—The Boundaries of Kashmir—Its Ruler—Designation of his Kingdom—Importance of the Situation of the Jamoo and Kashmir Territories—Form a Bulwark on Northern Frontier—Invasion of India from the North—Probable Results of an Invasion—Passes leading to or from the Happy Valley—Their Number—Authorized Routes from India—Country between Plains of India and Kashmir—The District of the Outer Hills—Its Vegetation—Its Inhabitants—The Dogrâs—The Region of the Middle Mountains—Its Character—Its Inhabitants—The Pahâris—Concluding Remarks upon these Tracts.

ON glancing at the map of the great continent of Asia, we find in the north-west of Hindustan that division of our Empire in the East termed the Punjab, "the country of the five rivers;" an extensive territory watered by the Indus and its great affluents—the Jhelam, Chenab, Ravi, Beas, and Sutlej—the widest expanse of the great plains of India, and a British possession since the year 1849, which saw the final downfall of the Sikh power. This extensive territory is bounded on the west by the Suliman mountains; on the east and south-east by the river Sutlej; and on the north by the Himalayas, the most elevated and stupendous mountain system in the world. Their ranges of snowy and rugged peaks, towering above the high table-land of Tibet—a giant mountain chain of an average width of 150 miles, and extending in length for over 1200 miles along the flat and fertile plains of our Eastern empire—form a natural and formidable boundary to these territories on their northern side. It is however to the northernmost portion of this immense mountain range that I wish more particularly to draw the attention of my readers; for here, beyond the rugged ridges that skirt the Punjab, whose snow-clad peaks are discernible by the traveller long before his arrival at their base, lies the country we are about to visit—the far-famed Vale of Kashmir, the 'Happy Valley,' the scene of the poet Moore's inimitable *Lalla Rookh.*

And Kashmir is a theme well worthy of a poet. Nowhere in Asia, nor even perhaps in the remaining quarters of the globe, can the parallel be found of such an earthly paradise; a paradise in itself as formed by Nature, but made doubly beautiful by its surroundings. For these are bare, rugged, and frowning rocks, a wilderness of crags and mountains, whose lofty summits tower to the sky in their cold and barren grandeur—a solitary and uninhabitable waste. Yet in the midst of this scene of unutterable desolation there lies spread out a wide expanse of verdant plain, a smiling valley, a veritable jewel in Nature's own setting of frightful precipices, everlasting snows, vast glaciers, which, while adding to its beauty by the contrast, serve also as its protection. Shielded from the cold and piercing blasts of the higher regions that surround it on the north, it is equally protected by the girdling mountains on its other sides, whilst its elevation places it beyond the reach of the fiery heat of India's sunny plains; and thus it exhibits, in the midst of a wide waste of desolation, a scene of almost constant verdure and perpetual spring. It is little surprising therefore that this terrestrial paradise, as it is often called, should enjoy the celebrity to which it has attained in all civilized countries, and its name have become associated with a high degree of picturesque beauty, something distinctive, if not unique in character. For, as Vigne justly remarks, "Softness mantling over the sublime, snugness generally, elsewhere incompatible with extent, are the prevailing characteristics of the scenery of Kashmir, and verdure and the forest appear to have deserted the countries on the northward in order to embellish the slopes from its snowy mountains, give additional richness to its plains, and combine with its delightful climate to render it not unworthy of the rhyming epithets applied to it in the East of

> "'Kashmir-bi-nuzir—without an equal;
> Kashmir-Junat-puzir—equal to Paradise.'"

Apart however from its acknowledged claims to picturesque beauty, Kashmir has others no less important, and equally interesting alike to the scholar, the antiquary, and the prospect-hunter; for its recorded claim to be considered a place of the highest antiquity will, I am sure, be conceded by any who have studied its history, and have seen or heard of the noble ruins, relics of past days, standing yet in various parts of the Valley, testifying alike to its former greatness and prosperity. With traditions coeval with the flood, its history is probably as ancient as any other extant, excepting always that of the Old Testament. And while mention is made of Kashmir in the Maha-Barat and other early Sanscrit works of the Hindus, as a country of eminent kings and learned men, it possesses its own historical records in a work entitled the *Rajataringini*, or *Raj Tarung*, as the natives call it, the history of its earlier dynasties, probably written by different authors and at different periods, but generally acknowledged by Oriental scholars to be the only Eastern history of any antiquity, and the only early Sanscrit composition extant to which such a title can be properly applied. Again, its very situation with regard to the neighbouring countries is sufficient to convince any one, if further proof were needed, that it must have been a notable place at a very early period in the world's history. The fame of its beauty, of its fruitfulness, of its wine, and of the loveliness of its women, must, at a very distant period, have spread among the inhabitants of Central Asia and other regions further north. And, on its other border, the people dwelling on the arid plains of Hindustan, descendants of the great Aryan race, the same original stock also of the Kashmiris, must soon, with their superstitious regard for places in any way remarkable as sacred to one or other of their gods, have learned to look upon Kashmir as a holy place, or paradise, a feeling that still holds good amongst India's teeming millions, being shared at the present day alike by Mohammedans and Hindus.

The very origin of the name of this noble province

is wrapped in mystery, and the derivation of the word Kashmir, or Cashmere, as it is indifferently spelt, has been the subject of much speculation, carrying us back to the very earliest days in the history of the world. Those familiar with the geography of the East must have remarked that the words Kush and Kash are of frequent occurrence in the names of places, and that not only in one locality, but in the various countries that together form the Eastern hemisphere. We find Kush in Arabia and Mesopotamia; and the Biblical term Kush was undoubtedly applied to that country known to the ancients as Ethiopia, 'the land of dark men,' the present Nubia, Abyssinia, and adjacent parts.

Kash, as the initial syllable of Kashgar, occurs in Central Asia; and the Hindu Kush, or Koosh, is the name of the range of mountains, the westward continuation of the Himalayas, separating Afghanistan on the south from Turkestan on the north; while Kushi again was the ancient name of that holy city in Hindustan now known as Benares. The repetition of the term in so many different places naturally leads to the inference that these various names have some common origin; and numerous and varied are the arguments set forth by the different Oriental scholars who have interested themselves on the subject, as to the source of its derivation. Confining ourselves to the country more immediately under our notice, Professor H. H. Wilson is of opinion that the word Kashmir is derived from Kashuf-mir, the country of Kashuf, the Mohammedan term for Kusyapa of Hindu history, the reputed grandson of Brahma, through whose instrumentality, at the command of Solomon, the Valley, then existing as a large lake, was drained of its waters. This is one of the earliest Kashmirian legends, and will be more fully noticed when treating of the geology of the Vale. Another derivation given is that from the Hindu word Kasyapa-pur—'pur' or 'poor' being a common ending to Indian names of places, signifying 'town' or 'city' and which, pronounced Kashup-pur, might have become in course of time converted into Kashamur and Kashmir.

The Emperor Baber in his *Memoirs* mentions the subject, and says, "The hill country along the upper course of the Sind or Indus was formerly inhabited by a race of men called Kas," and he conjectures that the country of Kashmir was so called as being the country of a people of that name. The natives of the Valley itself pronounce its name as Kushmir rather than Kashmir, and I have remarked the same fact amongst the inhabitants of India; and Vigne, probably led by this peculiarity, propounds an ingenious theory, which he states to be a not improbable origin of the name, if it came from the West at all, and which I imagine is equally applicable to other places in the East with the same or a similar prefix. It is as follows: "Cush was the son of Ham, and grandson of Noah (Genesis x.)—Cush begat Nimrod; he began to be mighty upon the earth." Nimrod is supposed to be identical with Belus, the beginning of whose kingdom was Babel, *i.e.*, Babylon, whence his name and power, and probably his descendants, must have spread over different countries to the eastward.

The general reader, however, I am sure will not care to pursue such an abstruse subject any further; as authorities differ, and enough has been said to prove on all hands the antiquity of the name, and therefore to certify the same fact for the country itself. We will, consequently, proceed to consider more particularly the Happy Valley and its inhabitants in their present condition, commencing with a brief outline sketch of the country itself—its geographical situation and surroundings, and the passes or routes by which ingress or egress are obtained.

Kashmir may be defined as a country consisting for the most part of a comparatively level tract of land, a wide vale or plain, embedded and set high in that portion of the mountain mass of the great Himalayan chain which skirts the north-western border of Hindustan, stretching between lat. 33° 15′ and 34° 35′ N., and long. 74° 10′ and 75° 40′ E. It is entirely surrounded by ranges of this stupendous chain; forming one large enclosed valley, divided into two unequal portions by the river Jhelam, which traverses its entire length, and having numerous glens or minor valleys, opening into it on every side from the lower portion of the lofty rocky wall by which it is environed. In form it is irregularly oblong, lying north-west and south-east; about ninety miles in length, with a width of twenty miles or even less at its narrowest, to twenty-five miles at its broadest part; with an area of 4,500 square miles, and an average height of 5,200 feet above the sea level. An irregular oval ring of mountains —as will be seen on reference to the map accompanying this volume—entirely surrounds and encloses this secluded region. Their ridges vary in height, and also in appearance. On the southern side we find that portion of the range known as the Pir Panjál, separating the Valley from the Punjab, with peaks varying in height from 8,000 to 15,000 feet, the sides of which are covered with dense forests, and their summits crowned in winter with pure and glistening snow. On the northern side the mountains are still higher, approaching in some cases even 18,000 feet; bare and rugged in appearance; their loftiest peaks being covered with a perpetual snow-cap. To all appearance, when surveyed from any eminence, the rocky walls of this prisoned valley appear to be unbroken and undivided. But such is not the case. There is one gap, and one only, in the rocky barrier. This is at the north-west end, where the river Jhelam, the Hydaspes of the Greeks, after collecting the drainage waters of the hills that surround the Valley, flows out by a narrow opening near the town of Baramula, and proceeds on its troubled course to become finally a deep and placid stream, as one of the five great tributaries of the Indus in the Punjab.

As regards its relation to surrounding countries, Kashmir is bounded north by Astor, Iskardo, and other districts of Little Tibet; east by Drás, Sooroo, Zanskar, and Ladák; south by Poonch, Naoshera, Kishtawár, Badrawár, and Jamoo—mountain states lying on the borders of the British districts of Jhelam, Gujerat, and Siálkote, in the Punjab; and west by Khághán, and the districts under our rule of Hazara and Ráwal Pindi. All these districts, excepting of course those mentioned as belonging to the British power, form together a kingdom either directly or indirectly under the rule of one ruler, known by the title of the Maharajah of Jamoo and Kashmir, one of our feudatories, and bound to us, if not from affection, undoubtedly by the ties of self-interest. He is a veritable 'king of the mountains;' for of such does his kingdom for the most part consist; and its several parts, inhabited by peoples of different races, and even of different faiths, possess no bond of cohesion other than the fact of his rule, and no simple name to embrace the whole dominion. On older maps it is usually designated by the term Golab Singh's Dominions; while the more modern group the various parts into one, and apply to it the title of Kashmir, a name derived from the far-famed country of which we are more directly treating, and which lies in its midst. This is a fact apt to be misleading to any one not thoroughly conversant with the geography and history of this part of the world; for Golab Singh has passed over to the great majority, and his son rules in his stead; while the designation of Kashmir should strictly be applied only to the Valley; but as yet no more fitting designation has been employed, although a recent author has suggested and adopted in his description of these countries the more comprehensive term, considered in relation to the ruler's title, of the Jamoo and Kashmir Territories.

In its relations to our rule in India the position of this kingdom, its physical and other characters, have an importance which its extent and general barrenness would scarcely warrant; for it constitutes a formidable defence, a rocky bulwark to our empire on its northern frontier, a natural obstacle against any foe proceeding from that quarter, and one which is said to be strengthened still further at the present time by the acquisition to the Maharajah, with the consent of our government, of the territory lying a little to the north-west, on the very borders of Turkestan. The passes of this territory the Maharajah has been instructed to guard during the course of our present hostilities with Afghanistan,* not so much against this enemy to our peace as to meet any eventuality which may arise, even at the most distant points on our frontier, in connection with the effacement of the Khanates of Central Asia by that grasping, unscrupulous, and half-civilized European power, our hereditary foe in the East, whose hitherto costly and barren conquests in the direction of our Indian empire, to the borders of

* Now satisfactorily concluded.

which they are rapidly approaching, can bear but one interpretation—the fulfilment of the dream of an ambition cherished for ages past. Were these designs once carried out, it would mean for us a surrender of the brightest jewel of our Imperial diadem of state; for the victors, its possession and enjoyment; and for the mild Hindu and the other inhabitants of Hindustan, who are no less directly concerned, the substitution of the just and impartial rule of their Empress-Queen for the so-called benign and fatherly rule of the White Czar, aided and enforced by Cossack whips and other Tartar devices. But the frontier of these territories is satisfactory for defensive purposes, and the river Indus supplements the great ranges of mountains, whose passes are long and difficult to traverse, few in number, covered with snow for the greater part of the year, and whose ruler, the Maharajah of Jamoo and Kashmir, is our friend and faithful ally. Hence I opine that to invade India on this side would be a wild and profitless undertaking; and granted even that a hostile force advanced through these mountains, and occupied the fertile Valley of Kashmir itself, which would afford them supplies, it would prove a precarious situation, unless they immediately passed out thence in sufficient strength to ensure a decisive victory over our troops on the adjacent plains of the Punjab. This would be difficult; for it would be only feasible for a lightly-equipped force to traverse these rough mountain parts. The paths to the Vale are few in number, and instead of glorious victory, more probably complete defeat would be their portion. Snow would in all likelihood cut off their retreat by the way they had come; while over the less lofty ridges of the ranges that skirt our border could the offended British legions cross, and in their might and power overwhelm and crush them before aid or succour could arrive from the North.

To return, however, to Kashmir, by which I mean, both here and elsewhere throughout the entire volume, to imply the Valley itself only; for although the other parts of the country which go to form the entire territory, so often, however wrongly, known by this name, are deeply interesting to the traveller, I did not myself visit them, and such information as I have gathered regarding them can have but incidental reference. We now come to consider the passes or routes by which ingress or egress to the Vale from or to surrounding parts is obtained. The well-known native historian, Abu Fazl, the minister of the great monarch Akbar, who has been termed the Oriental Sully, states in his work on Kashmir, which he several times visited in the train of his master, that there are no less than twenty-six passes leading into the Valley, and that an active mountaineer could enter it in many other places than by the regular routes; while Vigne describes as many as twenty. There will be no need, however, to enumerate the whole number, half of them being but rarely if ever used; and the following list, taken from Dr. Ince's reliable *Handbook*, will be sufficient, giving as it does the principal passes that are open for the whole or greater part of the year, some of course being closed in winter by the snow that falls in the higher regions.

PRINCIPAL PASSES INTO THE KASHMIR VALLEY.

Situation.	Name.	Height.	Whence.
South	Pir Panjál . .	11.400	Bhimber and Rájáorí.
"	Báramula . .	?	Marri, Poonch, and Abbotabad.
"	Ferózepore . .	?	Poonch, and Rájáorí.
"	Banihál . . .	9.200	Jamoo.
East	Marbal . . .	11.570	Kishtawár and Chamba.
"	Margan . . .	11.600	Maroo Wardwan and Sooroo.
North	Zozilá, or Drás	11.300	Drás and Ladák.
"	Rájdiangan .	11.800	Gurais, Tilail, and Little Tibet.
West	Tootmári Galli	?	Karnár.
"	Naschau Galli	?	Karnár.
"	Patti Khair .	?	Dráwar.

The four first of these are the passes leading into the Valley from the plains of India, which therefore only concern us at present; the remainder lead to or from countries that I did not visit, and consequently do not come within my present design. And furthermore, it is only upon the two first named that I need dwell at length. They are the routes by which I passed in and out of the country, and which would surely be selected by any traveller from India to the Valley, the Feròzepore route offering no greater advantages; while the Banihál, leading from Jamoo, may be termed a private road, being forbidden to the ordinary wayfarer, and kept open for the sole use of the Maharajah and his family, whose custom it is to visit yearly the Happy Valley, the fairest part of his whole dominion. The two first roads from India may again be subdivided into four, and these are the only authorized or public routes, it being forbidden to travel by any other unless under special permission obtained from the Supreme Government. They are as follows:

1. The Gujerat and Pir Panjál Route.
2. The Gujerat and Poonch Route.
3. The Ráwal Pindi and Marri Route.
4. The Ráwal Pindi and Abbottabad Route.

These routes will all be found on the map that

accompanies this volume, as also in the Appendix. At the risk even of being thought a trifle wearisome, I must now proceed to give a short description of the two principal, on account of their own interest, and as a prelude to the romantic scenery and delights of the Valley itself. On the Gujerät and Poonch route I need not dwell, as it is a branch road merely, and taken only as a rule if the Pir Panjál Pass is blocked by snow. The same applies to the Abbottabad road, which is of very little interest, and rarely used, except by officers from that or other frontier stations in the Punjab.

But before proceeding let us take a cursory glance at the country that they traverse, its inhabitants, and other details connected therewith, and the necessary arrangements that must be effected to insure the safety and comfort of the traveller on his long and mountainous march. As already stated, the Valley of Kashmir is entirely encircled by mountains, those on its southern side being the range of the Pir Panjál, separating it from our own Indian possessions, the plains of the Punjab, over which we must make our way in order to reach the goal of our journey. Before arriving, however, at the loftiest heights of this mountain mass, there is an intermediate district, rough and rugged in character, sparsely inhabited, poorly cultivated—small patches of land only being fit for tillage—and with scrub forest and bare rock as its more prominent features. To this tract has been applied, by an author to whom I am much indebted for the following remarks, the appropriate term of 'The Outer Hills;' and to that further towards the higher parts of the mountain, 'The Regions of the Middle Mountains.'* It is an interesting country, alike from the difference in its physical features, its vegetation, and its people. This is most marked on the Gujerat and Pir Panjál route than the others named, excepting, of course, the Banihal Marri, the starting-point of the so-called road lying on ground corresponding in character to the second tract, and with a very small space of the first-named separating it from the plains of the Punjab, the road to the Vale passing for the greater part of the way up the valley of the Jhelam.

Let us first take the district of the Outer Hills, so called, the skirts of the mountain mass of the Himalayas, which with a greater or less width edges its course along their entire length, and in the territories which concern us chiefly has an extent of 150 miles, with a width varying from

* *The Northern Barrier of India.*—F. DREW.

fourteen to thirty-six miles, in a line drawn from the river Ravi on the east to the Jhelam on the west. These hills slope up very gradually from the plains, continuing to a height of nearly 2,000 feet—their sides clothed with forests of small trees, for the most part of the acacia species, with various shrubs as an undergrowth—and then fall a little, constituting for several miles a rough broken tract of land redeemed only by an occasional small valley or 'dûn.' On these favoured spots are the towns and villages of the inhabitants, and the cultivated ground, which bears crops similar to those obtained in the northern parts of India; the climate and general vegetation of the belt being also pretty nearly of the same character. It is, however, to the inhabitants of these parts that the greatest interest attaches, for among these hills live the race of men called Dogrâ, headed by the Maharajah of Jamoo and Kashmir, himself of the same stock—the ruling class over the whole of the territories that comprise the so-called Kashmir kingdom; and here also is to be found the capital town of Jamoo, for many years the chief head-quarters of the members of their royal line. A branch of the Aryans, and settling in the hills that skirt the Punjab, while their brethren went still further and colonized the greater part of India, they approach, in appearance, character, and habits, the Hindus; modified of course by their somewhat isolated position, and their naturally altered mode of life. In appearance, especially among the higher classes, they may be termed decidedly good-looking, of a much fairer complexion than the Hindus of the plains, slim-made, and, if not very muscular, active and strong for their size, which is considerably less than that of Europeans. They profess the Brahmanical faith, or its heterodox form known as the Sikh religion, and are divided into castes in nearly the same way as the Hindus generally; out of which number the Brahman and the Rajput divisions are the principal. The first-named is the highest caste, the same as in other parts of Hindustan; but in these quarters they are more numerous, perhaps, and more inclined to take to various occupations, other than learning and combined religious devotion; while the Rajputs are the same as they always are—the traditional aristocratic class, supplying both warriors and rulers to the state. There are various other castes, chiefly confined to members following one occupation; and there are low-caste people, and even outcasts, among them, as in the plains. Without entering into this subject further, I may remark that the despised classes differ in colour, being darker, and have other characters distinguishing them from the higher ones, and are supposed to be descendants of the original non-Aryan inhabitants of these hills. These observations apply more directly to that portion of the Outer Hills lying between the Ravi on the east and the Chenab river. Further west, between this boundary and the Jhelam, a somewhat different race is found, professing the Mohammedan religion, who are often termed Chibhâlis; but, as a rule, they are not very strong in their faith, and differ little in other respects from the Dogrâs, of whom they are a branch, converted to the Mohammedan form of worship in years gone past.

We now come to the Region of the Middle Mountains, on the road to the Valley, and which, on the same authority already quoted, is given in these provinces as including the country around Bhadarwáh, Kishtwár, Ramban, Rajaori, and Poonch, the two last places that are passed on the Pir Panjál route, and Muzafarabad, near to the Ráwal Pindi and Marri road. The whole of the area of this tract, which is about forty miles in width on the east, lessening to a third of that distance about its centre, and spreading out again indefinitely towards the north-east, is occupied by hills, approaching sometimes to the height of even 12,000 feet, with deep hollows formed by the rivers that ramify in these mountain masses, and which again have a number of valleys spreading out in every direction from their courses, but all small in size, and closely hemmed in, and surrounded by rocky walls. The height of this region gives a different character to the vegetation, as compared with that of the Outer Hills. Forests of Himalayan oak, of pine, spruce, silver fir, and deodar are to be seen on the slopes of the mountains; while the root and grain crops are scanty, both from the nature of the ground and climate; for in winter snow falls all over this tract, though rarely, if ever, in the district just described. The inhabitants of the Middle Mountains are again very different to the Dogrâs, or to other Hindus generally, although followers of the same religion, excepting to the north-west, where Mohammedanism is followed, the people of that locality having been already described under the head of Chibhâlis. More to the eastern portion of this tract the people have remained Hindu in faith, manners, and customs, retaining caste and other peculiarities; but differing in appearance, dress, and mode of life from the inhabitants of the country nearer the plains. They are a strong, active race, with a powerful physique, pronounced and not unpleasant features, mostly having a nose markedly hooked—a peculiarity to be noticed in the inhabitants of the Valley itself, as also among the hill tribes on our north-western border. No distinct name exists for this particular race (or rather races; for there are many subdivisions of tribes), and they have no general appellation amongst themselves. They are usually termed Pahâris, meaning mountaineers, a comprehensible name, and as good as any other; so, for convenience' sake, in speaking of the inhabitants of this region on our march to the Vale, we will so designate them, excepting always the true Kashmiris, many of whom are to be found in the villages as we approach the termination of our journey.

Such then, in brief outline, is the country and its inhabitants, lying between the Indian plains and the lofty wall of mountain ranges, on the other side of which is to be found the Valley itself, with an appearance and a people totally distinct, a country which must be traversed by long and wearisome marches before arriving at the smiling plain beyond. And although this sketch is very incomplete, and gives but an imperfect idea of the territory as it really exists, still I trust it will convey a general impression of the nature and surroundings of this mountainous tract to those of my readers who are interested in the subject, and who are ready and willing to accompany our journey as detailed in the following chapter.

CHAPTER II.

The Routes to the Valley—The Seasons for Visiting the Valley—Hints to Travellers—Supplies—Servants—Money—Conveyance—The Gujerat and Pir Panjál Route—Called the Imperial Road—The Road to Bhimber—Bhimber—Its Former Rulers—March to Saidabad—The Aditak Range—Mogul Seraies—March to Naoshera—The Kaman Goshi—The View—Marches to Changas and Rajaori—Fording the River—Rajaori—Thanna Mundi—Baramgalla—The Rutten Pir—Wooden Bridges—March to Poshiana—Its Houses—The Pir Panjál Pass—View from the Summit—March to Hirpur—The Town of Shupiyan—Further Road to the Vale—Ramoo—Arrival at Srinagar—The Ráwal Pindi and Marri Route—Hill Carts—Marches to Daywal and Kohála—The River Jhelam—Chatar Kalas—Marches to Rara, Tinali, Gharri, and Hatti—Chakóti—Ooree—Road from Poonch—Ooramboo—Naoshera—Town of Báramúla—By Water to Srinager—Srinagar.

OF the four authorized or public routes to the Valley already mentioned, that which is known as the Gujerat and Pir Panjál is decidedly the grandest as regards scenery, as well as the most interesting on account of its historical associations, which take us back to the palmy days of the Great Moguls. It is also the most convenient to all travellers from any part of India, excepting those stationed higher up in the

Punjab. Gujerat, the starting-point, is only some seventy-five miles from Lahore, and now connected with that city by the Northern State Railway, while Rawál Pindi, the starting-point for the other route, is 100 miles further on.

Such being the case, this is perhaps the most frequented road, and one that should most certainly be selected, either in proceeding to or returning from the Valley; for, although a little harder to travel than the other, it is well worth the extra fatigue. In my own case, when in the summer of 1875, accompanied by my wife, I made the tour to the Happy Valley, we proceeded by the second, as we were anxious to stay a short time in the cool climate of Marri before commencing the journey after our grilling in the Fortress Gwalior, my then station, and also to avoid the heavy rains, as it was then the month of July, and these falling at that time in the higher mountains cause the rivers to be so swollen on the other road as to render them almost entirely impassable.

We returned, however, by the Pir Panjál route, and being thus equally familiar with either, I will essay a short sketch of the march over these highways to the Vale, prefacing it with a few observations as to certain specialities regarding travelling in the Himalayas. As regards the best season for visiting the Valley, and for travelling over the mountain roads that lead to it, opinions differ. Most people prefer the first three months after the passes are open from the winter's snow, from about the middle of April to the middle of June. The next best time is perhaps from the middle of August to the end of October — the period intervening between these dates being the least preferable, particularly for the journey, as it is the season when heavy rains fall upon the mountains. As regards the other months of the year, it hardly need be said that ~~few or~~ no Europeans visit the Valley in the winter; in fact I believe that to do so is forbidden by the Kashmir government.

It need scarcely be observed that there are no hotels or shops to be met with on the different roads to the Valley. It becomes therefore necessary for the traveller to procure and carry with him nearly everything requisite for his support and comfort on the journey. There is certainly at every stage or halting-place a bungalow, or some kind of shelter to be found, set apart for his use. But he will most probably find need for his tent on the way; for many of these rest-houses are mean and dirty, and, possessing but limited accommodation, are often found already filled on his arrival by others who have preceded him. Although there are no shops, still certain supplies, such as wood, milk, eggs, fowls, and vegetables, are procurable at most of the villages, where native servants will find all they require; but for their masters anything required in excess of what is mentioned above must be procured at Gujerat or Marri, according to the route selected. No luxuries will be obtainable after leaving these stations until arrival at Srinagar, where several good shops for European stores are kept by Parsees and others.

Among the other articles requisite, both for the march and when moving about the Valley, there are of course a tent and tent-furniture, such as carpet, table, chairs, bedstead, bedding, bath, &c., all of which should be made so as to take to pieces or fold up, and are generally procurable in the bazaars of the stations from whence the start is made. Another tent will be found necessary for the accommodation of the servants, as well as cooking things, plates, cups, and glasses, and also washing and ironing requisites, and other articles which they need, taking care, however, not to allow them to have all they say they want, as in that case their requirements would be endless. As to servants, opinions differ; but from experience I can say, the fewer the better; for if numerous, they are a great incumbrance, being perfectly helpless out of their own country, unless accustomed to marching or mountain travelling. For a bachelor, two will be found sufficient. We only took four, and found the number ample to attend to our wants; but we possessed a treasure in our head-man, or butler, Esau, whose name will be familiar to those who have read *Our Life and Travels in India*, and who on this trip took the general direction of affairs, as he was accustomed to do in our Indian bungalow. To carry all the *impedimenta* enumerated above, coolies, mules, and ponies are required, and they are to be found at all the halting-places, and are paid four annas each man, and double that amount each baggage animal for the day's march. Certain rules to be observed for procuring them, as also some useful hints to travellers on this journey, will be found in Appendix iii. It occasionally happens that fresh coolies or mules cannot be procured at one or two of the halting-places, so it is always advisable to ascertain that fact before payment is made to those in employ. If none are at hand or willing to proceed the original ones must be retained to go onwards the next day; and the only way to insure their services is to defer paying them at all, or giving them a fourth only of their wage until their services can be dispensed with and fresh ones taken on in their place. To pay one's way on the journey it is necessary to take a supply of rupees and smaller coins, enough to last until arrival at Srinagar, when no difficulty will be met with in replenishing the purse; for the tradesmen at that city act as bankers, cashing treasury drafts, or even cheques, for a small percentage.

Both the roads to the Vale about to be described are rideable nearly all the way; at certain rough places only is it necessary to dismount, and sure-footed ponies are to be found at most of the halting-places, although many of the hardier sex prefer walking all the distance. For ladies who do not wish to ride, there is the dandi. This consists of a light cane seat and foot-piece attached to an oval wooden frame, with a short pole at each end which rests upon the bearers' shoulders—the same bearers, four in number to each dandi, being procured at the starting-point, and engaged for the whole tour.

Being thus prepared with servants, baggage, and coolies, and mules to carry the supplies, and in the case of officers of the army, or civilians in government employ, with the necessary pass or permit, not required by other travellers, we will now start on our mountain march over the great Pir Panjál. The distance from Gujerat to Srinagar is about 176 miles, covered in fourteen marches, a day's march varying, according to the nature of the ground and the position of the villages on the road, from ten, or even fewer miles, to twelve and fifteen. As before stated, the Gujerat and Pir Panjál route was the one by which the Mogul Emperors passed on their way to the Valley, and numerous were the journeys of the members of that royal line from the time of its annexation by the great Akbar, in the year 1587. From the fact of these monarchs using this route, it was, and even is yet, termed the Imperial Road, and the traveller of to-day cannot fail to be reminded of their former presence, and recall their ancient grandeur, when he observes the ruins of the magnificent serais, or inns, and other buildings, erected at intervals along the road for the accommodation of the monarch and the numerous retainers that accompanied the Court.

On leaving Gujerat, a pretty little station on the Grand Trunk Road, about seventy miles above Lahore, the capital of the Punjab, we proceed to make for Bhimber, a distance of twenty-eight miles, which can be easily covered in one day, as it is over the level plain, either by stage-cart or 'dhooly dâk.' This is by far the most satisfactory way of commencing the journey; for after leaving Bhimber a country is entered upon in which civilization in the shape of wheeled vehicles, or luxurious modes of travelling is left behind, and the dandies for ladies, and ponies for the sterner sex take their place, serving their purpose very well, except in certain parts of the passes, where I certainly consider the wayfarer's own lower limbs the safest and most reliable means of progression. The road to Bhimber from Gujerat is easy enough to travel, and the country passed over presents the usual features of the landscape as seen in the Punjab,—a continuous plain, at certain seasons of the year green and cultivated, at others dusty and sandy, and devoid of all vegetation save that presented by a few clumps of trees and shrubs, which stand about the vicinity of the small villages, or rather collections of mud huts, pretty plentifully dotted about this part of the Indian lowlands. No objects of any interest are met with on the road, which, as one nears the town, becomes sandy and broken up by numerous water-courses, the whole country looking as if it had been in former days a huge marsh, now dried up; for nothing in the shape of vegetation is to be remarked over the whole expanse, save some tufts of reeds and long coarse grass.

The town of Bhimber is of considerable size, containing a number of houses—some of fair proportions—and built of rough unhewn stone, mud, and wood, situated just at the edge of the plain so lately traversed on leaving Gujerat; and surrounded, except on its southern side, with low hills densely wooded—a portion of the Outer Hills, already described.

At the present time it presents a somewhat desolate and forsaken appearance; a contrast to what it must have done in former days, when it was the capital and residence of an independent Rajah, whose last representative, Sultan Khan, came to an untimely end. Having acted in opposition to the then powerful Sikh ruler, Runjit Singh, in his designs on the Valley, he was conquered and taken prisoner by the Lion of the Punjab's Lieutenant, Golab Singh, who directed and actually carried out the barbarous proceeding of destroying his sight, by means, it is said, of a silver bodkin made hot by friction. The unhappy Rajah, after this torture, was kept in close confinement until his death, in the year 1830; his dominions becoming incorporated with the Sikh State, and at its disruption passing into the hands of his executioner, Golab Singh, and becoming a part of the Jamoo and Kashmir territories as existing at the present day. The ruins of the old palace are yet standing, as also those of a Mogul serai, with the remains of a fort; and on the summit of a hill, some few miles distant, is the castle of Amur Gurgh—'The immortal fortress,'—built by an uncle of the present ruler, and well worthy inspection if time can be spared.

The first stage from Bhimber and the next halting-place is Saidabad, a distance of fifteen miles, which will be found sufficient for one day's march, since now the difficulties of the journey fairly commence. The road at first is fairly good; but one has to cross within the distance of a few miles a small river no less than eight times, on account of its numerous windings. The guide-books state that its bed is rough and rocky; an assertion I can well sustain, having experienced practical proof of its condition from a heavy fall in the stream, caused by the pony I was riding tumbling headlong over a boulder at one of the crossings. About six miles from our destination a range of sandstone hills, called the Aditak, has to be crossed, the ascent being made by a rough, steep path of about three miles in length. The summit of the ridge, which is about 1,000 feet above the level of the plains of the Punjab, commands in fair weather a highly picturesque and extensive view of the country we have left—the Saidabad valley, the continuation of our journey, lying spread out in front with a background of mountains, the loftiest peaks being those of the Pir Panjál range. The descent is easy; a winding path about a mile long leads us to the bottom of the ridge, and continuing across some fields by the right bank of a pretty little river for nearly four miles, turns to the left, and, after fording a small stream, conducts to the village, where a good stone bungalow has been erected for the accommodation of travellers.

There is nothing to be seen here except the Samani serai, a building still in fairly good preservation, supposed to have been built by Akbar, and consequently one of the earliest erections of this sort along the royal road. As all these serais are pretty similar in construction, one description will suffice, and that in a few words, for there is nothing very particular about them, being similar to the usual so-called caravanserais met with all through the East. They generally consist of a large square stone building, of which the architecture is usually Saracenic in character. After passing through a massive doorway and gaining the centre of the building, which is uncovered, they will be seen to be formed entirely of four large walls, oftentimes twenty feet or more in thickness, with deep niches, like cells, formed out of their depth, all with the openings towards the roofless square enclosure which they surround. These niches formed the separate accommodation for those who sought their shelter; and the four walls and the enclosure, as described above, often form the entire structure. This however is supplemented in the larger and grander ones by the addition of a suite of rooms raised above the level of the ground, which, with other chambers and a 'hamâm' or bath-room, no doubt formed the royal quarters for the accommodation of the Mogul and his family.

Naoshera, about twelve miles from Saidabad, is usually the next march, and the road for the first few miles is easy to follow, continuing along the banks of the river, across fields and low grassy hills. About halfway we come to another small range, called the Kaman Goshi, which is formed of sandstone similar to the Aditak, crossed the previous day, and may with it be regarded as the stepping-stones to the great Himalayas. The path to the summit is about a mile long, and mostly over bare, slippery, dull-coloured rocks, and its scenery and general surroundings are very much like parts of Scotland. A very fine view is obtained after the pull to the top of the ridge is surmounted; for the whole open plain or valley just left lies spread out, a green and smiling expanse, offering a marked contrast to the surrounding ranges of mountains, which in front appear to cover the entire country as far as the eye can reach, range after range, with the Pir Panjál for a background. The descent is easy, the path being generally smooth, and on arrival at its foot a pleasant walk of another three miles brings one to Naoshera, a compact stone-built town situated in an open plain on the right bank of the Tawi river.

There is not much to be seen, however, either in it or in the vicinity, so leaving the town the following day the traveller proceeds to make for Changas, a village lying about fourteen miles away, the road to which is not very difficult to traverse, leading as it does along the comparatively level ground of the valley of the Tawi river, a narrow but pretty glen, bounded on each side by low and beautifully wooded hills. The village of Changas is on a plateau on the right bank of the river, and a quarter of a mile distant is a bungalow, the best on the road, in my opinion, which commands from its verandah what is said to be the most magnificent view obtainable of the Pir Panjál range. This I can well endorse, and we saw it to perfection; for a heavy fall of snow the previous day had covered the peaks, which stood out boldly and well-defined against the clear blue sky, and, bathed in a roseate flood of light from the rays of the setting sun, afforded a spectacle of grandeur and beauty not to be easily effaced from our minds.

The next march leads us to Rajaori, and here, too, the fourteen miles of road are comparatively easy to overcome, passing over a not very steep or rough path along the right bank of our old friend the Tawi, which has to be forded just opposite the town in order to reach the usual encamping-ground and rest-bungalow, situated on the left bank of the swiftly-flowing stream. The crossing of the river at this point is oftentimes no easy matter, particularly if there has lately been a heavy fall of rain in the mountains, which at first for some little time renders it even totally impassable. Such had been the case when we essayed its passage, and this was the cause of my passing perhaps the most miserable quarter of an hour I ever experienced; for the stream was icy cold, deep, and rapid, flowing over a bed exceedingly rough and full of large loose boulders, and to cross this quarter of a mile of water, for such was about its width, swollen as it was with the late rain, we had to hold on to each other tightly to prevent being swept away by the force of the current. Forming a living chain by grasping each other's hands, myself, servants, and coolies went stumbling over, the water being sometimes up to our chins, at other times scarcely covering our knees; while its loose stony bed made but a poor surface to stand on. The coldness of the water, coming as it did from the snowy mountains, most effectually deprived us of the little breath we could spare after our exertions to maintain our erect position and progress forwards, and to add to my misery and anxiety, I had the unpleasant reflection that if the twelve men, who just ahead of me were swaying and tottering from side to side under the burden of the dandi, were not staunch and strong enough to preserve their footing, the miserable spectacle would be presented of its overthrow, and probable drowning of its occupant, the dear companion of my journey, neither I myself nor any of my following being able to render the slightest assistance to obviate such a dire calamity. We fortunately, however, experienced no such untoward misfortune, and all reaching safely the opposite side continued our way, wet but rejoicing.

The town of Rajaori, also sometimes called Rampore, is the largest met with along this route, and is most picturesquely situated on an angle formed by the junction of the Tawi and another small river, the waters of the former washing the stone walls of the palace, a building which rises directly from its bed. Low-lying hills covered with jungle surround the town, which is of fair size, with houses built of wood, mud, or brick, and contains several noticeable places, either within its walls or in its vicinity, such as temples and other buildings. Formerly the seat of an independent Rajah, it was a place of some considerable importance, and in its palmy days has seen grand sights and entertainments, given by the members of its ancient line of sovereigns, which is said to have dated from the eleventh century, to the Moguls and their retinue, when they halted here on their way to the Valley. But these days have departed never to return. After the fall of the Mogul dynasty, the state lost little by little its possessions, and being finally seized by Golab Singh in 1847, became merged into the Sikh dominions, and subsequently, like Bhimber, into the Kashmir Raj; while the members of the family of the last of its rulers sought British protection, and are at the present time settled in the tea-growing district of Kangra.

On leaving Rajaori the road to Thanna Mundi, the next halting-place, a distance of fourteen miles, is easy to march on, and pleasant throughout, passing along the valley. This, however, with the river becomes narrower and narrower, until merged in the Rutten Pir range of mountains, which rises straight in front. The valley through which we pass is fairly fruitful, and rice in considerable quantity is raised on ground terraced and made into fields, which are flooded at the proper seasons with water from the river that flows through its midst. On arriving at the village we find ourselves surrounded by much bolder scenery; for we have now entered upon the Region of the Middle Mountains, and the hills already crossed sink into insignificance when contrasted with those which overshadow this place, and whose sides, covered with forests of pine, spruce, and fir trees, form the third intervening range between the Pir Panjál and the point of departure.

In the next march to Baramgalla, a short but hard one of ten miles, this Rutten Pir range has to be crossed, a piece of pretty rough mountain travelling. The road to the Vale known as the Poonch route, and which is utilized when the passes in front are deep with snow, may be said to commence here. It branches off about a mile beyond Thanna, and, passing through the town from which it takes its name, proceeds on to join the Marri route, as will be seen by reference to the Appendix. The road after leaving Thanna, for the first mile or so, still continues along the side of the Tawi, which now is only a small stream, as we are nearing its source, at the foot of the range we have reached, and which has to be surmounted on the way to our next resting-place. It is hard work to gain the summit, the path being very rough and uneven at places; but when once surmounted, a magnificent view is the reward; for the top of the Rutten Pir stands 8,300 feet above the sea level, commanding an extensive tract of country, while looking north-eastward there are grand views of the Pir Panjál and adjacent mountains. The descent is equally steep and rough as the ascent, and one is not sorry to reach the village, which is close to the base of the ridge, near a stream, and entirely shut in by spurs of the mountains around, adding to its picturesque beauty in summer, but not serving much towards its protection in winter; for it is stated that at that season of the year snow lies about here to the depth of fifty feet. Just before reaching the village we had to cross the stream which runs near, and which is spanned by a bridge similar in construction to all met with in Kashmir, consisting of large logs of deodar or Himalayan cedar wood stretched from bank to bank, with rough planks and brushwood laid across them to form the platform.

The next march is to Poshiana; and to reach this place one has to follow the course of the river Sooran, which flows in an exceedingly narrow valley. For several miles the only road—on account of the steepness of the hills that hem it in—is over the loose stones of its bed; and as the stream has numerous alterations of course as it nears the cliffs on either side, it has to be crossed and re-crossed no less than thirty times in a distance of five miles over the little rickety primitive bridges described above. After leaving the stony track of the stream, about a mile or so this side of Poshiana, the path leads up its right bank, and a stiff pull of some hundreds of feet up the hillside brings us to this extraordinary place—a small village, the highest in the valley, and inhabited by Kashmiris.

The houses are built almost entirely of mud, on the precipitous hillside, rising tier above tier in some places; sufficient level ground for their construction having been hollowed out from the side of the mountain, against which they lean. Their roofs are flat and smooth; and if a tent has to be pitched for one's accommodation, as there is no rest-house available, it has to be put up on one of these roofs, for no other level piece of ground sufficiently large for the purpose could be found within some distance of the village. These flat roofs seem to serve another purpose as well as a protection against heavy snow; for I remarked that, as darkness drew near, the sheep, goats, and fowls were driven on to them up a species of rough ladder, or rather inclined plane of planks with cross-pieces, which was removed when they were all safely housed for the night over their owner's head, who was enabled to sleep in peace, knowing that his flocks and his herds were, as far as he could provide, in a measure secure against the attacks of wild beasts; in this locality pretty plentiful, but rather shy of approaching the habitation of men.

The next march is to Aliabad serai, and the distance eleven miles, but nearly sufficient for one day, for it is in this march the chief pass on the route, that of the Pir Panjál, is crossed; and that of itself is a pretty stiff climb. After leaving Poshiana, the road first contours to the base of the valley. At the upper end the ascent to the summit of the pass commences, which is reached by a steep, narrow, boulder-strewn path, cut in zigzag form out of the mountain side. The path is fairly good, but in places decidedly rough, over large rocks and loose stones; and it remains a marvel to me how the ponies and mules, often heavily laden, pass up and down, springing like cats from rock to rock. Progress upwards is necessarily slow; but with ordinary expedition, the top of the pass can be gained in something under four hours from leaving Poshiana, from which it is distant about six miles.

In ascending we pass successively through the different stages of mountain vegetation; and on nearing the summit, the pines, the firs, and shrubs have vanished; for we have arrived above the limit of forest growth, and nothing is around us but stunted grass, rocks, fallen stones, and, on the highest parts, unmelted snow. From the summit of the pass, which is a comparatively level piece of ground, with lofty walls of mountain masses on either side, standing at an elevation of 11,800 feet above the level of the sea, a magnificent prospect unfolds itself. It is one truly grand. On either side rise mountains, their peaks soaring aloft to a height in some cases of between sixteen and seventeen thousand feet. Straight in front the whole of the country, with the ranges already crossed, their valleys and their silvery streams, lies spread out as a picturesque panorama of rare and exceeding loveliness. Beyond again, as a dim grey expanse, are the plains of India, as far as the eye can reach, until lost in a hazy mist; and if the air be sufficiently clear the minarets of the capital of the Punjab can be discerned, a distance of 130 miles. From the summit a gradual and easy descent over a grass-covered plateau, like a mountain meadow hemmed in by walls of rock, a glen of five miles long by half a mile in width, brings one to Aliabad serai, which is nothing more than one of those usual places of shelter to the traveller, standing alone in its solitude, and deserted for the greater part of the year, when it is completely inaccessible through snow.

From this desolate region to Hirpur, the next stage, the road passes along and above the stream, which dashes wildly over the rocks, and with hills rising on either side forms a narrow valley, widening out, however, as we approach our destination; while the hills, their sides covered with forest trees, become mere hillocks compared with those to which we have hitherto been accustomed, and barely interfere with what is now obtainable—the first view of the far-famed Vale itself, so eagerly looked for, so gladly welcomed.

Deferring however for the present any description of the Valley, we will proceed on our journey, and make for the next halting-place—the town of Shupiyan, a large place, and the great commercial depôt of Kashmir and the Punjab, distant about eight miles from Hirpur, and reached by an easy road along the right bank of the river. From this town the further road to the capital lies north, about twenty-seven miles, and it can be easily reached in two marches. The village of Ramoo is the usual halting-place for the night, and the following day an easy ride of eighteen miles over a smooth and level road, planted with poplar trees on either side for a greater part of the way, brings us to Srinagar, when crossing the bridge that spans the river we make our way, weary with mountain travel, to the usual encamping-ground, rejoicing however in the fact that the toilsome marches are over, and the promised land, the Happy Valley, yea, even its capital, safely reached at last.

Regarding the other route into Kashmir from India, that called the Ráwal Pindi and Marri road, a few words will suffice; for it does not offer such magnificent scenery or other objects of interest to render it so attractive as the one just described, although it is picturesque along most of its way, a distance of nearly 200 miles, and as the travelling is easy, and there are no formidable mountain ridges to cross, the town of Srinagar can be easily reached in fourteen, or even half that number of marches. It is usual to proceed direct from Ráwal Pindi, a large civil and military station in the Punjab, about 100 miles from Peshawar, to the hill-station of Marri, distant forty miles, either by stage-cart or dhooly-dâk. If the latter is chosen, the travelling is easy and pleasant, but slow, and the quicker mode of progression is usually selected; namely, the cart. This, drawn by two horses, covers the ground in grand style, and is besides good for the liver; for the road being rough and hilly, the vehicle guiltless of springs, and the pace a gallop, one gets plenty of exercise; the nearest approach to anything like it in my experience being a long ride on a particularly rough-stepping horse. From this favourite sanitarium, the road, smooth and down hill, along the side of a picturesque valley, brings one in about ten miles to the village of Daywal, where there is a good bungalow to rest in for the night.

Kohála is the next point, a distance of ten miles, and over a similar road, being for the first five an easy descent to the river Jhelam, along the right bank of which the route now lies all the way to Srinagar, the rapid, roaring, rushing torrent being ever present on the daily march. Kohála itself, a small village, needs no description, and we proceed to make for Chatar Kalas, eleven miles off, situated in the Kashmirian kingdom, which is gained soon after leaving the first-named village by means of a suspension-bridge across the river Jhelam, the boundary between it and British territory. For nearly the first three miles the road follows the course of the river, with a fair ascent all the way, then, striking into the hills, it passes first over some pretty level ground and next over some steep gorges, when the rest-house is reached, standing on a plateau overlooking the river, and at an angle of the bed of a wide mountain torrent, which here joins the Jhelam. This rough and stony bed, like most others met with in the journey, is fordable nearly all the year, and is seldom very full or impassable, except just when the melting of the winter's snow sets in. Some excellent fishing is to be obtained about here, the mahseer being found of a very large size, varying between thirty and forty pounds weight, and affording some good sport before being brought to bank.

From this place to Rara, distant between ten and eleven miles, the road crosses the stony bed of the torrent noted above, and then, ascending, follows the side of a hill overlooking the river for about half the distance. Two or three miles more, over undulating ground, brings us within sight of our destination, towards which the road gradually descends; and after an easy walk of some two miles the rest-house is gained, most pleasantly situated on a level spot just above the rapid Jhelam.

Tináli, the next stage, is some thirteen miles distant; the road following the course of the river with some very steep ascents, over passes led up to by pathways constructed in a series of steps, made by laying logs of wood across, and filling in with earth. The rest-house is within a short distance of the river, at a sharp bend in its course; this, being full of small rocks, causes a seething and foaming of the water, which on its rapid onward course becomes a rushing, roaring torrent, magnificent to witness. From this place the road, passing chiefly over comparatively level ground for eight miles, brings us to a long, wide plateau, upon which we find the rest-house of Ghari—our halting-place for the night.

The next stage to Hatti, some ten miles or so, is a very pleasant journey; a good deal of level ground being passed over among fertile fields and charming scenery, and amidst a quiet which is appreciated after the continuous roar of the river, which has hitherto been the accompaniment of the daily march.

On leaving Hatti—a small village high up on the mountain-side—for Chákoti, fifteen miles distant, the road first descends with a sharp gradient to a stream; crossing which a steeper ascent has to be accomplished, literally up the face of a hill, by zig-zag paths. There are a number of ascents and descents on this march, and several streams to be crossed, most of which are, however, bridged; but it is a fatiguing journey, and one welcomes gladly the bungalow, which is come upon suddenly, just after rising from one of those water-courses, most pleasantly situated, overlooking a scene of fertility and prosperity in the form of wide-spreading fields of corn and rice.

From Chákoti to Ooree is sixteen miles, the roughest and most fatiguing march on this route;

still along the valley of the Jhelam, the path passing for the most part up and down numerous ravines. In the first two-thirds of the stage the hardest work has to be done; the last few miles being pretty level, ending at a small mountain stream, from the bed of which a steep ascent brings one to a large open plain, where the rest-house of Ooree is placed, overlooking the river.

At this place the cross-road from Poonch—mentioned a few pages back when describing the other route—joins this; and, continuing our way, after a rather steep descent to the bed of a stream, and a similar ascent, the path passes along the left bank of the river through most beautiful scenery to Ooramboo, about ten miles off, where an excellent bungalow has been lately built; and the next march past the village of Naoshera brings us to Báramúla, by a road easy and pleasant. This is the termination of the tramp, for it conducts us into the Happy Valley; and, once arrived at Báramúla, the choice is offered of proceeding either by water or by land. The first is usually selected; for it is two long marches on to Srinagar; and besides, the journey by boat, which takes about twenty hours, is by far the pleasantest, passing across the Woolar lake—the largest in Kashmir—through which the

Jhelam flows. Some miles further on the city becomes visible; and soon the encamping-ground is reached—the same to which I have already conducted my readers by the other route. Having thus safely arrived in the heart of the country we came to visit, we will now turn our attention to the Valley itself—its history, people, manners and customs, and other matters relative to this most picturesque and romantic land.

CHAPTER III.

Arrival at Srinagar—The Encamping Ground for European Visitors—The Babu—Courtesy shown by the Maharajah to Visitors—The British Officials in Kashmir—The Takt-i-Suliman—Its Legend—Stone Temple on its Summit—Panoramic View of the City and the Valley—The Dal Lake—Mountains Surrounding the Valley—The River Jhelam—The Land in the Centre of the Valley—The Kareewahs—European Character of the Scenery—Physical History of the Valley—Formerly a Lake—Volcanic Agencies in its Formation—Evidences of former Lacustrine Condition of Valley—Formation of Kareewahs—The Desiccation of the Valley.—Legend respecting its Desiccation—Vigne's Theory of its Desiccation—Early History of Kashmir—Wilson's Essay on the Hindu History of Kashmir—Its Native Kings—Its Mohammedan Rulers—The Chákk Family—The Great Moguls—Its Afghan Rulers—Ranjit Singh—Decline of the Prosperity of Kashmir—England's Opportunity for its Acquisition—What might have followed—Its present Ruler—Form of Government in Kashmir.

HAVING arrived at Srinagar, the first care of the visitor to the Happy Valley is to find a suitable place on the ground set apart for the use of Europeans, to pitch his tent, and settle quietly down for a few days, to recover from the fatigues of the mountain journey, and also to explore at leisure the city and its environs before proceeding further afield. And this is not a difficult task; for a more suitable spot for the purpose could scarcely be found than that selected, a little above the city on the right bank of the river, facing which some good bungalows have of late years been erected for the accommodation of strangers. There are two ranges of these buildings. The lower one, commencing about a quarter of a mile above the bridge, is intended solely for the use of bachelors. It consists of ten bungalows, standing in three gardens or orchards, built of wood, each containing four rooms; and in these the unmarried visitors take up their abode, themselves supplying of course the necessary furniture, while those who arrive later, to find them all occupied, pitch their tents in the vicinity, and if desirous of exchanging a canvas house for one of stouter material, a desideratum in rainy weather, must wait for a vacancy, the privilege of occupancy ceasing on leaving Srinagar after the lapse of a few days. The same law holds good in regard to those sacred to the use of the Benedicts and their families. This range, usually styled the married range, consists of sixteen houses of similar construction, except a few larger ones built of brick, situated in a large garden called the Moonshi Bagh, where excellent ground is obtained for those who prefer their own tents. When we visited Srinagar, we had at first to live in our tent, every room being occupied. Well do I remember our arrival, and the putting up of our travelling house. For we arrived late in the evening, after a long and fatiguing march from Gulmarg, and it was pitch-dark when we reached the encamping ground, which we at first had some little difficulty in finding. And further trouble was in store for us, wet, cold and hungry as we were, the pitching of a tent being no joke when it has to be performed by the light of a single tallow candle stuck in a lanthorn, and by the aid of a lot of unwilling natives, weary and half-famished. However, it was done at last, and we turned in and enjoyed a good night's rest. We were lucky enough to secure the reversion of two rooms in one of the bungalows, which we entered upon in a few days. There we remained for the rest of our stay, enjoying them much; for although, perhaps, not so romantic, yet dwelling under a good roof is decidedly preferable to living in a tent. Soon after arrival you are favoured with a call from the Native Agent deputed by the Kashmirian government to afford aid and information to the European visitors, and very willing and obliging we found him. His office is not very far distant, where he can usually be found; but he generally attends every day at the visitors' quarters, ready to give his assistance in the clearing up of such knotty points as the prices of articles, rates of fares, and the endless disputes between the Indian servants and the natives of the country.

A curious, but a very polite, custom prevails in Kashmir, that on the day following one's arrival, the Native Agent, attended by a number of servants, in making his first visit, presents an offering of food and fruit, and a sheep or a goat from the Maharajah, at the same time bidding you welcome in his name to the capital of his country. This politeness of the ruler of the state to strangers is frequently extended not only to the living, but to the dead; for if an English officer is so unfortunate as to come to his death during his stay in the Valley, this attentive prince, to show his sympathy with the melancholy event, usually sends a shawl of price to wrap the body in before burial. In addition to the Kashmir official mentioned above, there are three European officers detailed annually by the Indian government for duty during the season in the Happy Valley. These are, a civil officer or Resident, who is the medium of communication between the visitors and the native officials, and who also possesses jurisdiction over all British subjects during their stay; a medical officer to attend to their bodily wants, and a chaplain, who performs divine service every Sunday, to attend to their spiritual needs. To these three officials a residence is assigned between the two ranges of quarters already described, and on them it is advisable to call soon after arrival. Politeness demands it, and often necessity compels it.

Being now comfortably established, and recovered from fatigue, our first care will be to ascend some height whence a good general view of the Valley and the city can be obtained. This can easily be effected; for, as if made for such a purpose, immediately behind the married range of houses stands a hill known as the Takt-i-Suliman, or 'Throne of Solomon,' at an elevation of 6,250 feet above the sea, or a little more than 1,000 feet above that of Srinagar. Whence its name I know not, for certainly we possess no record of that well-known personage of Bible history ever establishing his regal seat on this elevated mound. But it is curious as showing how often in the East we meet with the names of those familiar to us in sacred history, in native legends and literature, or in actual reality—as in the reputed grave of Noah and his sons at Ajudhia, near Faizabad—that there are two eminences in this part of Asia that bear this designation. Why or wherefore the name of Takt-i-Suliman was applied to that elevated mountain of the Sulimani range* is difficult to say, as native legends do not allege any wonders performed by that monarch anywhere in its vicinity. Whereas, on the one to which we shall shortly direct our steps, Solomon, the great prophet, the mighty magician, is supposed by all good Mussulmans to have taken his stand during the progress of the desiccation of the Valley, carried out by his orders through the means of a spirit or spirits rendered subservient by the Almighty to his will.

Let us now ascend this hill, which has also another name to that already mentioned, being styled by the Hindus the Sir-i-Shur, or 'Head of Siva.' To effect our purpose we pass out of the orchard at the back of our quarters, and climbing over a low earth wall that surrounds it, find ourselves in a small field, through which a path runs which conducts on to the road just behind the village of Drogjun, on the western side of the hill, and close to the gate of the city lake. Here the path to the summit of this isolated hill commences, and the ascent is made with ease in the space of half-an-hour; for a series of stone steps, made by order of the late Maharajah, extends nearly all the way, rendering it comparatively easy to the most indifferent pedestrian. On the top of the hill, which is of trap formation, stands an interesting relic of bygone days, which carries us back 2,000 years in the history of the country; for this fine old stone temple, which rises on the very summit of the Takt-i-Suliman, and which is yet in a good state of preservation, was, according to all authentic accounts, erected by Jaloka, the son of Asoka, that well-known Indian prince, and supporter of Buddhism, who flourished some 200 years before the Christian era. In form a cone of nearly thirty feet in height, with a proportionate base, it is elevated upon an octagonal stone platform, about twelve feet in height, on the eastern side of which is a fine flight of steps leading from the ground to the door of the temple, formed of slabs of limestone highly polished, the same material entering into the composition of the whole building. Its interior is circular, fourteen feet in diameter, with a flat roof, supported upon four stone pillars, and in its centre stands a quadrangular platform, supporting a lingam of black stone, which testifies to the diversity of faiths followed at different periods within its walls.

To face page 60

From a photograph by Mr. H. Simpson.

Stanford's Geogl. Estabt.

ANCIENT TEMPLE ON THE TAKT-I-SULIMAN, SRINAGAR

Originally a Buddhist temple, like the country, later on it became Mohammedan, and was converted into a mosque; while the presence within it at the present day of this emblem of the worship of Siva, testifies that it has also been utilized by the followers of the Hindu religion.

Turning our attention now to the object for which we have more particularly undergone the trouble of ascending the mount, we find that beautiful indeed is the panoramic view presented to the eye of the spectator from the summit of the Takt-i-Suliman, which, from its situation in the centre of one of the sides of the Valley, commands nearly its whole length and breadth. Commencing at the very foot of the hill, we see the city of Srinagar extending for two miles along both banks of the river Jhelam, presenting a curious assemblage of gable-ended houses of diversified architecture, many with their roofs overlaid with earth, green with grass, and other plants. Interspersed amongst the ordinary dwelling-houses are seen many larger buildings of a different order, with pinnacles, and occasionally glittering roofs of metal, mosques and other edifices devoted to religion. The palace of the Maharajah, with its golden-roofed temple, rises on the left bank of the river, which as it flows through the city is of an average breadth of about eighty-eight yards, spanned at different places by seven wooden bridges, easily to be counted from our present stand-point. A number of canals or water-courses meandering in divers directions, and roads or paths, their sides planted with poplar or other trees, in leafy avenues, with some small patches here and there of cultivated ground, complete the picture of the capital of the Valley and its immediate surroundings. Separated by a wide gully from the Takt, and frowning down on the city, stands the Pandu Chákk mountain, and extending from this to the northward a precipitous but verdant range circles round the next object that attracts our attention, the 'Dal' or city lake, and, sweeping round the greater part of its circumference, continues into a far higher range, becoming part of the greater one that surrounds the Valley. The lake, whose shores are about a mile from the base of these green and lofty mountains, and on the north-eastern side of the city, lies spread out, a tranquil sheet of water of five miles in length by about two and a half in width, its edges fringed with willows, poplars, and other trees; while the thicker masses of foliage that attract the eye are those that form the famous gardens of the Shalimar and the Nasseeb Bagh, or 'Garden of Bliss.' Another green spot is the Isle of Chenars, or the 'Silver Island,' situated about the middle of the lake; and in the centre of its southern portion is to be seen its companion, the Sona Lank, or 'Golden Island.' Numerous little villages, surrounded with trees and rich and cultivated land, on the edge that borders the city, complete the *coup d'œil* of the lake, that portion of the Vale more particularly described in *Lalla Rookh*, and to a more minute inspection of which we will return a little later on. Taking now a more extended view, we glance over the greater part of the Valley itself, and from our elevation can trace the vast mural cordillera that forms its boundary on every side. In front is the lofty range of the Pir Panjál, continuing on the south with the mountains of Kishtawar, and on the north-west into the still loftier and snowy peaks of Durawur and the Dardu country. Northward, the gigantic Haramuk rises in majesty; while that important range of mountains that bounds Kashmir on the north-east stands in all its grandeur, with peaks over 20,000 feet high, and with snow that gives rise to many a glacier. Several isolated hills, in fact small mountains, are scattered over the Valley. Those of Shupiyan and Islamabad are prominent objects on the south. more than twenty miles distant; and looking northward we perceive the rounded summit of Aha Thung, concealing the beautiful Manasbal lake; and nearer to the city, on its northern side, the Harri Parbat, its summit occupied by the fort erected in days long past by the great Akbar, to command the capital of the province so lately added to his dominions. The course of the broad and beautiful Jhelam, and its windings as it approaches the city from the southward, are clearly to be traced, as well as its further progress throughout the entire length of the Valley; that larger streak of water on the north side is the Woolar, or 'great lake,' through which it passes to make its exit at Báramúla, some few miles further on. By the banks of this river lies a flat plain of rich, open, arable and meadow land, varying in width from two or three to fifteen miles, formed like the usual alluvial flats by the deposition of sediment on the water overflowing its boundaries at flood-time. Beyond this rich and savannah-like tract, and filling up the rest of the space in the centre of the Vale, are those open, raised downs or plateaus, of alluvial or lacustrine material called kareewahs, often separated from each other by deep ravines, formed by the different watercourses in their passage from the mountains beyond to their destination, the river. Some of these downs are dry and bare; others, again, richly cultivated, being irrigated by small streams; while some, particularly on the southern side of the Valley, are joined to the lower spurs of the Pir Panjál range, and bear forests of pine. Beyond this tract of raised downs, and approaching nearer to the rocky boundary of the Valley, lies a rugged country, intersected by ravines and furrowed by rushing and raging torrents; and beyond again are the first slopes of the mountain barrier that hems us in, covered on the south-western side with dense forests of pine and deodar, and with grass only on the more northern aspect. Innumerable villages and isolated farm-houses are dotted about all over the landscape. It is, indeed, one that reminds us of home; and we can hardly realize that only just beyond that chain of mountains which appears so near lie the hot and arid plains of India. For although in a general view we see kareewahs, corn-fields, rice-grounds, meadows, and morasses, occupying the centre of the Valley, with mountain slopes and yet higher ranges beyond, the aspect of the scenery is European in character. It has not the verdure of the tropics; and although the trees in many instances differ from those found in

Europe, at a distance this difference is not remarkable, and as its glens, glades, and streams are truly Alpine, nothing is wanting to complete the picture of a country Asiatic by situation, but with natural characteristics most thoroughly European.

Regarding the physical history of the Valley, the traveller Vigne remarks that, taking a general view from any elevated spot, the walls of the Valley, in consequence of the disposition of the mountains near Báramúla, appear, excepting from very near the place itself, to be unbroken and undivided, enclosing a large hollow, which at first sight gave him an idea of its having been originally formed by the falling in of an exhausted volcanic region. This theory he states, however, is not confirmed by an examination in detail, which tends to produce abundant evidence as to the truth of the tradition, that this smiling Valley was once a lake, a large inland sea, one of the deepest and most extensive that ever existed on the surface of the Asiatic continent. That volcanic action had some share either in the formation of the original lake or its subsequent desiccation is most probable, and is to be traced in the mountains around the Vale. These are chiefly basaltic in character, their usual formation being a beautiful amygdaloidal trap, while in many places, more especially on the southern side, we find the surface composed of grey compact mountain limestone, in which marine fossils and shells are often found imbedded. This limestone is usually to be seen contorted and twisted in every possible direction, having apparently been uplifted and broken through by the trappean rock from beneath, testifying to the force of the convulsions of nature in former days. Actual and positive proof, too, exists in the present to prove that volcanic action is still at work beneath the surface of the Valley of Kashmir; for shocks of earthquake are not unfrequent, although there have been none of late years equalling in severity that in June, 1828, when great loss of life and property resulted, as also was the case in a similar visitation some fifty years anterior to this; while, going back some few centuries, we find it mentioned that similar phenomena occurred in the year 1552.

The chief evidences of the former lacustrine state of the Valley are undoubtedly the masses of shingly conglomerate, the remains of beaches, deposited in horizontal layers upon the distorted limestone strata, and on the faces of the kareewahs or eminences that form so striking a feature in the topography of the Valley, whose characteristic flat and uniformly

F 2

even surface can only be attributable to their having been submerged for ages beneath the still calm waters of a deep vast lake. With reference to this subject, and to the formation of these kareewahs, General A. Cunningham writes as follows, and affording as he does a clear, concise argument as to the correctness of the lake theory of the former condition of the Vale, I cannot do better than quote his own words.* He writes as follows :

"The rocky cliffs below Tattamoola, and about sixteen miles below Báramúla, rise almost perpendicularly from the river Jhelam to a height of 300 and 400 feet, and in some places that I noticed the bare steep cliffs were not less than 800 feet above the stream. As the height of the Jhelam, near Tattamoola, is about 5,000 feet above the sea, the whole of Kashmir must have been submerged by the waters of the river before the wearing down of these cliffs. The level of the Kashmirian lake would have been about 5,800 feet above the sea, and from fifty to 100 feet above the kareewahs or isolated alluvial flats now remaining in Kashmir. The high level land of Martand was probably not submerged, but the horizontal beach-marks are still quite distinct on the limestone cliffs above the

* CUNNINGHAM'S *Ladak.*

cave of Bhaumajo and the holy spring of Bawun. Above Ramoo-ke-serai, on the Shupiyan river, the kareewah forms a bank about 100 feet in height, in horizontal strata of different kinds. The uppermost twenty feet are composed of stiff alluvial soil; the next twenty feet of rolled stones and loose earth, and the lowermost sixty of indurated blue clay. The last must have been deposited by the lake in its state of quiescence, but the middle stratum could only have been formed by the first grand rush of waters, on some sudden burst of the rocky barrier below Tattamoola, and the uppermost would have been deposited by the subsiding waters as they reached the newly-formed level. Then, as the rocky bed was gradually worn down, the different streams worked new channels for themselves in the former bed of the lake, until the present kareewahs of Nonagar, Pampur, and Khanpur were left, first as islands in the decreasing lake, and eventually as long flat-topped hills in the midst of the open plain, just as we now see them."

As to the period in the world's history when this lake existed, and what manner of people inhabited its shores, we possess no authentic proof; nor do we as to the time of its desiccation, or whether this process was due to the effect of a sudden formation.

of an outlet through the Báramúla Pass, or its drainage was the work of time. According to the history of the country, as laid down in the *Rajataringini*, its drainage is said to have been sudden, but this book, like all other works of a similar nature relating to the East and its early days, is a mixture of truth and fiction—a certain proportion of truth mixed up with a larger mass of ridiculous and fabulous accounts of the works of the gods and genii, and legends concerning them.

In the *Rajataringini* mention is made of the existence of a large lake on the present site of the Valley, from which account it may be inferred that it was supposed to have been left from the deluge, its desiccation being due to supernatural agency, as explained in the following and still-credited legend: "The country was entirely covered with water, in the midst of which resided the demon Jala, or Dewala Deo, the spirit-god who preyed upon mankind. It happened that Kashuf, the son of Marichi, and according to some the grandson of Brahma, visited the country, lived in pious abstraction upon Mount Sumer or Soma, and, turning his attention to the desolate appearance of the earth, enquired the cause. The people told him of the residence of Jala Deo in Sati Sar, and his predatory incursions.

Kashuf lived a thousand years in austerity upon the hill of Naubudan, near Hirapur, in consequence of which Mahadeo (the great god or creator) sent his servants Vishnu and Brahma to expel the demon. Vishnu was engaged in the conflict for one hundred years, and at last opened the mountains at Báramúla, by which the waters were drained off, and the demon was exposed, taken, and slain, whence the country is called Kashuf Sar, or 'the lake of Kashuf.'" Such is the legend as given in the Hindu history of the country; and a nearly similar story is entertained by the Mussulmans, who, as I have already remarked, affirm that the draining of Kashmir was performed by the prophet Suliman (Solomon) through the aid of the same Kashuf, who they believe to have been a 'gin,' or spirit, and the attendant of that monarch.

No actual proof exists that the valley was suddenly converted from a lake to the condition in which we now behold it; and in fact, taking into consideration the evidences afforded by such an examination into the matter as any skilled geologist is capable of, the results obtained rather tend to prove the contrary, and are well set forth by Vigne himself, a skilled and most accurate observer. He fully believes in the tradition of the natives as to the valley having been originally a lake of between 300 and 400 feet in depth; but holds that its drainage was the work of time. From observation he inferred that the basaltic ridges around Kashmir had been raised from beneath and through extensive beds in the deep ocean, and that the salt water of the original lake must have gradually disappeared under the influx of the numerous fresh-water streams from the mountains. Further, that the mountains near the Báramúla Pass, which would otherwise have opposed the exit of the waters altogether in that quarter, were rent asunder at the same time; other barriers, however, being left a little lower down sufficiently elevated to collect the alluvium, or its greater part, carried by the flood down the Pass, which became choked with deposit, preventing further escape of soil, and thus accounting for the great quantity of earth still in the Valley as compared with neighbouring countries. Gradually the waters from the newly-formed lake formed a deeper channel for themselves, and occasional sudden subsidences in its level were probably formed by the carrying away of some part of the obstacles in the Pass, evidence of this fact being afforded in certain parts, where the limestone has the appearance of having been worn into a succession of shelving-beaches. As time went on, and owing to the gradual sinking, the level of the lake became lower, the waters that once fed it poured themselves into the bed of the river Jhelam, which gradually wore itself a channel in the lowest part, and thus concentrated, worked through the remaining obstacles in the Pass, and became the rapid, rushing torrent we now see leaving the Valley, and the present means of carrying off the superfluous waters always pouring down into it from the mountain sides, and thus preventing a return to its former condition as existing in pre-historic times.

When we come to consider the actual history of this now beautiful country, we are met at the outset with the usual difficulties attending all researches into Eastern histories. Historians there have been who in treating of the subject carry its history back to the day of creation, and assign to it the honour of having been visited by the first living man, even descending into details, affirming that this event occurred after the Fall. Moses, Seth, the Deluge, Solomon, and other characters and events, known to us through the word of holy writ, are freely commented upon in connection with the subject of its early days, and are detailed in the *Rajataringini* and other works.

Space will not, however, permit me to dwell upon what may have been the events of its earlier history; for it is a subject of abstruse speculation, and would fill a volume of itself.* Rather let us confine ourselves to a cursory glance at the somewhat better authenticated shreds of history that we possess relating to its earlier days, and, without entering into dry details, take a slight sketch of its condition and of its rulers, from the time when its interest became merged into that of the neighbouring country of Hindustan, up to facts existing in the recollection of many of my readers.

The country of Kashmir, then, appears from all accounts to have been ruled from a very remote period in the world's history by a long succession of native princes, sometimes Hindu, and sometimes perhaps of Tartar origin. In Professor Wilson's essay on *The Hindu History of Kashmir*, founded on the before mentioned *Rajatarangini* (and of which he states that, although its early part is fabulous, it gradually approaches consistency, until from about A.D. 600 the chronology is perfectly accurate), a list of kings is given who are said to

* Any one who wishes for a more general acquaintance with the ancient history of Kashmir should read Professor H. H. Wilson's "Essay on the Hindu History of Kashmir." (*Trans. Asiatic Soc.*, vol. xv.)

have ruled after a line of thirty-five princes whose names have been forgotten. Amongst others in this list we find the name of Khagendra, supposed to have flourished some 500 years before Christ, and who it appears was the first monarch who founded a city in Kashmir. Following this ruler came several others, the last of whom leaving no heir, the throne reverted to the family of its former kings, and devolved on Asoka, descended from the paternal great uncle of Khagendra. The name of Asoka will be familiar to those conversant with the history of India, as it is generally admitted that this strenuous upholder of the then new faith of Buddhism ruled also over a great part of that country, about 250 B.C., and left tokens of his existence in the form of those chiselled letters on stone, still extant at Allahabad and elsewhere, and usually termed Asoka's inscriptions or edicts. His son Jaloka succeeded him, and erected, as already stated, the temple on the top of the Takt-i-Suliman. This brings us to about two centuries before the Christian era. Following him came several princes, probably of the same line, one of whom, Abhimanyu by name, is stated to have introduced about 75 B.C. the Hindu religion into the country. A succession of Tartar princes are said to have ruled over Kashmir during the last century before Christ and for long years after. However, we will not dwell on the subject of its earlier history further, as the greater part of it is but mere supposition, except to mention that a reference to Wilson's notice of Kashmir, or Prinsep's tables, informs us what power and importance Kashmir must have attained when it was under the dominion of its Hindu monarchs. Still it was reserved to the Mogul emperors to raise it to that eminence of station, the account of which has been transmitted to the present day. Passing therefore over several centuries, we will now arrive at the year 1000, the time of the life of the Sultan Mahmud of Ghazni, whose invasion and conquest of the greater part of Hindustan marks the period when the authentic history of that country may be said to commence. This great and warlike prince, the founder of the Mohammedan empire in India, found time in the intervals of his expeditions into that country, which are said to have been no less than twelve in number before he established a permanent footing, to make several similar predatory incursions into Kashmir. In the two first he did not succeed in his object; for, owing to the season being far advanced when the attempt was made, joined to imperfect knowledge of the passes, his army suffered defeat, many lives being lost. He was, however, more fortunate in a later attempt, and about the year 1015 he took possession of the Valley, holding it and the surrounding mountains for some considerable time.

The Mohammedans do not appear to have established at that time a permanent footing in the country, which reverted again to its Hindu kings, under whose rule it most probably remained until the beginning of the fourteenth century, when most authorities agree that it was invaded from Tibet, and its Hindu king, Sena Deva, flying the country, was superseded by the son of the monarch of the land of the invaders, who took the name of Sadarudin on his accession to the throne of the coveted Valley. From his time to the present it is easy to trace the history of the country and its line of independent Mohammedan kings, its Mogul emperors, and its Pathan rulers, until, conquered by Ranjit Singh, it became a part of the Sikh state, on their downfall a British possession, and finally was handed over to the family of the present ruler.

First, as regards its line of Mohammedan kings, Sadarudin was succeeded, as was often the case in those days in the East, by his prime minister, Shah Mir, who took the name of Shumshudin, and who, ascending the throne in the year 1341, is usually considered as the first true Mussulman king of Kashmir, his predecessor's conversion to that faith not being fairly authenticated. His successors were his sons Jamshed and Ullahudin, his grandson, the bigoted Shahabudin, who was succeeded by his brother Kutabudin, the father of the execrated Sikunder But-Shikan. This latter personage, one of the most notorious iconoclasts of history, made it the business of his life to destroy all vestiges of any faith except his own, and to his exertions in this direction is due the sorrowful fact that all the ancient temples and other buildings in the Happy Valley are to be seen at the present day existing only as a mass of ruins.

In the year 1423 came the best of the line, Zinulabudin, or Badshah, the great and good king, whose name is yet reverenced throughout the country over which he for more than half a century exercised his beneficent sway. To him the Valley owed much of its future prosperity, for he introduced the arts of weaving, paper-making, and other industries peculiar to the country and its inhabitants, and still pursued at the present day, as will be shown a little later on. His great grandson, Mohamed Shah, succeeded him, but his title to the throne was disputed by his uncle, Futteh Shah. There now occurred civil strife of many years' duration, the final consequence of which was the entrance of another political party upon the scene, their advancement to power, and as the result the consequent downfall and extinction of that line of sovereigns, the descendants of Yuftan, king of Tibet.

This new ruling race was the old warlike tribe of the Chákk, the ancient warriors of Kashmir, at that time a powerful race, but hitherto held in subjection by the Mohammedans, until the family dissensions broke out and enabled one of their number, named Kaji, to seize the opportunity afforded by these intestine struggles, and free his country from the yoke of a foreign invader. He commenced to reign about the year 1536, and his martial talents were quickly called into play; for soon after his accession the country was invaded by the Kashgarris, who are said to have penetrated some considerable distance into the Valley before their final defeat. About this time also the fame of the country of Kashmir attracted the cupidity of the Mogul family, then established as rulers over a greater part of Hindustan. It is more than probable that members of that royal line had previous to this attempted its conquest; and on the authority of Abu Fuzl, it may be mentioned that the generals of the Emperor Baber, invaded the Valley in 1494, but that the natives were sufficiently powerful to cause their retreat. A few years later, however, in the time of his son Humayun, we come to more authentic details; for this monarch, on his second attempt, took possession of the coveted country in 1540, the first having been successfully resisted by Kaji, the Chákk king. Mirza Hyder, a relation of the Mogul, and to whose generalship he was largely indebted, was appointed the governor of the province, which appointment he held, however, only for a short time; for an insurrection broke out, and he was defeated and slain. This gave the opportunity for the Chákk family to return to power, which they held through the successive reigns of Ghazi Khan, Yusaf Shah, and his son Yakub Khan. During the time these princes held rule over their native country, many were the attempts at its subjection made by the Moguls, Tartars, Kashgarris, Turks, and other enemies. Fortune, however, did not favour the invading arms until the year 1587, when the last of the line, Yakub Khan, after a brave and protracted resistance, was finally defeated by the armies of the great Akbar, who annexed it. From that time to the present day the Valley has always continued under a foreign yoke.

For over a period of a century and a half Kashmir remained a portion of the Mogul Empire, its affairs being administered by a resident 'Subadar,' or governor. Frequent were the visits of the members of the House of Delhi to this, their fairest province. Akbar is said to have visited it three times, while Jehangir and the beautiful Nurmahal resided there during the summer for several years in succession; and the death of the first-named took place on one of his journeys thither, at Baramgalla, a place we have already visited on our way to the Vale by the Pir Panjál route. His successors also visited it often, and all have left evidences of their former presence in the country; for with the exception of the ruins that denote its earlier history, all the remains of gardens, groves, baths, fountains, and palaces, that are still to be observed in the Valley, owe their origin to the lavish and magnificent tastes of the different members of that truly Oriental regal family.

The decline of the Mogul Empire, hastened by the capture of Delhi by Nadir Shah, in 1739, occasioned changes in the Valley; and after several abortive attempts on the part of its governors to establish an independent rule, it was annexed in the year 1753 by Ahmed Shah Abdali, the successor of the conqueror of Delhi, and included in the Dourani Empire, which extended in those days as far as the capital of the Punjab. From 1753 to 1819 it remained a portion of this empire, being governed by Pathan governors, whose rule was neither mild nor beneficial. It was with a feeling of satisfaction that the inhabitants of the country welcomed the change of masters which occurred in the month of July of the latter year, when the forces of Ranjit Singh defeated the Pathans, and it became a part of the Sikh dominions, remaining so until their downfall, when, falling into the hands of the British by right of conquest, it was by them transferred to the family of its present ruler. Exchanging thus, after nearly five centuries' experience, Mohammedan rulers for Hindu, Kashmir continued to be governed pretty much as usual by representatives of the Sikh monarch, who never visited it himself, and whose principal object in its possession seemed to be the squeezing out of it as much revenue as its falling fortunes would allow. Thanks to the numerous invasions, and the rapacity of its conquerors, the Valley of Kashmir was not the same rich and fruitful country of former days, and the little that was left was soon exhausted by the oppression of the minions of the lion of the Punjab. Natural causes had also some little share in the devastation of the Happy Valley; for in 1824 occurred the terrible earthquakes, followed a few years later by destructive floods, and an epidemic of cholera so severe and so general that it is said that 20,000 died of it in the capital alone. All these things naturally militated against its recovering the prosperity it enjoyed, by all accounts, in early days, when the number of its inhabitants was ten times the present population, disease and starvation, together with emigration, having terribly reduced the census. Brighter days are perhaps yet in store for this fair province; but what it might have been when, after the dissolution of the Sikh empire, it passed into our hands, if our government had allowed it to remain a part of our Eastern possessions, I can form a very good opinion. The author already quoted, who visited the Valley during the time of Ranjit Singh, appears even then to have been struck with the idea of its becoming at some future time a British possession, and states that its acquisition would be looked upon as the accomplishment of the one thing needful for the consolidation of the British power in Northern India. This augury as to the future is now in a measure fulfilled, although not actually by the occupation of the territory in question, but by our subsequent conquest of the Punjab, and present administration of that country and the parts adjacent, which, including Kashmir, are tributary to our rule, and retained subservient to our wishes. But it is not only to its political or strategical importance that our attention should be directed, but to the benefits that the English rule (which with all the best intentions in the world can never be approached by any native prince) would have conferred on the country. For, to quote the words of Vigne, "It is to the arts of peace that this fine province will be indebted for a more solid and lasting, though less gorgeous, celebrity than it enjoyed under the Emperors of Delhi. The finest breeds of horses and cattle of every description may be reared upon its extensive mountain-pastures, where every variety of temperature may be procured for them; its vegetable and artificial productions may be treated with British skill and capital in such a manner as to ensure an excellence equal to those of Europe, and superior to that of the neighbouring countries; while the tools of a Cornish miner may bring to light the hidden treasures of its iron, lead, copper, and silver ores." All this is as true to-day as when he wrote, and from actual observation I can endorse his every sentence, and see the chance we wantonly threw away of doing what seems impossible in India otherwise—colonizing a portion of our Eastern possessions. It is well known to all conversant with Indian affairs that, unfortunately for us, our countrymen cannot settle down in India and bring up families, like our representatives in our other colonies. The climate and other reasons forbid it. If the attempt was carried out it would result in such a deterioration of our race as would bring them below the level of the people we rule over; and although it has been suggested that the scheme would succeed in the Hills bordering our provinces, yet I question its feasibility; the climate there, although better than that enjoyed on the plains, is yet not a perfectly natural one to Europeans; while the space that could be cultivated for their support would be limited indeed. Now, no such factors exist against the colonization of Kashmir by us or by any other European nation. The climate is all that can be desired; sufficient land exists, which, properly tilled and cultivated, would support any number; while water is good, and distributed abundantly all over the Valley. In fact, nothing is left that could be desired to form, by the means of our retired soldiers and others, a miniature England in the heart of Asia—a stronghold in time of war, held and guarded by the loyal sons of Albion, ever willing and ready to shed their own and children's blood in defence of their home, and the other provinces that together form our Imperial dominion in the East.

But it was not to be. The huckstering spirit that so often pervades our national policy, and which caused the great Napoleon to apply to us the term of a nation of shop-keepers, was dominant in this case; for, relinquishing all the advantages that accrued to us from its possession, the supreme government sold this fair province to the Rajah Gulab Singh for the paltry and insignificant sum of seventy-five lacs of rupees, £750,000 in our money, and the treaty by which it was assigned, known as the treaty of Amritsar, and dated 16th March, 1846, will be found set forth at length in the Appendix by such of my readers who feel interest in the subject. The prince to whom this transfer was made has already come under our notice in connection with the town of Bhimber, and the death of its former ruler; but as the founder of the present royal family of Kashmir, we will take a short glance at his history. Descended from an old Dogrâ family, squires or dependents of the ancient Rajahs of Jamoo, he quarrelled with his rightful master, and after remaining a few years in the service of the ruler of Kishtawur, became, through the influence of his brother Dhihan Singh, a trusted officer of the Maharajah Ranjit Singh, the great Sikh monarch. Obtaining a command, he proceeded against his hereditary master, who, flying his capital without resistance, gave the opportunity to Gulab of annexing the state in the name of the Sikh ruler. Further distinguishing himself in many of the hill wars then taking place, he was rewarded by Ranjit with the sovereignty of his own home, holding the rajahship of Jamoo in fief under the court of Lahore. This occurred about the year 1820, and for some time afterwards he was fully occupied in consolidating and even extending his power. With a firm hand he put down lawlessness in his own dominion, and made it a model state; and being ever ready to employ intrigue rather than force, he took advantage of the dissensions always present among his neighbours, the petty hill chiefs, and little by little confiscated their fiefs. Having effected the conquest of Ladakh and Baltistân, there remained but one country to covet, the country of Kashmir, and that soon fell into his hands. During the war between the Sihks and the British, Gulab Singh kept himself entirely aloof from Lahore politics, and after our victory appeared on the scene as mediator between the two parties, acquiring the confidence of our government to the extent exemplified by the cession of the Valley. Dying in 1857, he was succeeded by his son, the present Maharajah Ranbir Singh, who was at that time a young man of twenty-seven years of age. Residing for the greater part of the year at Jamoo, he annually visits the Valley, and sees for himself the state of affairs in this part of his kingdom, which is administered by a governor, as in former days. He is what may be termed, in comparison with the generality of Eastern princes, enlightened, studious, and fond of the society of the pundits and other clever men. He is eminently religious, and in faith is an orthodox Sikh, being generally considered at the present time the head of this sect of the Hindus. He is also a great encourager of education, liberally supports all religious works, and, according to his lights, desires to act fairly and honestly to his people in this part of his dominions, aliens as they are for the most part both in race and creed. If the same could be justly said of many of his advisers, the future of Kashmir would, perhaps, look brighter;

but with the best intentions in the world, the actual ruler of many an Eastern state knows little of what is really transpiring, self-interest and self-aggrandizement being usually more powerful factors in the deeds and acts of their servants and representatives, than actual devotion to the good of their country, and faithful duty to their master.

In ancient days the province was divided, for the purposes of government, into two portions, which were again divided into thirty-six 'pergannahs' or hundreds; but within the last few years it has been organized upon another plan, having been separated into six 'wazarits' or districts, which are again split up into a number of 'tehsils' or parishes. Over each district a 'wazeer' or deputy commissioner holds sway, subject of course to the head governor, who takes his orders directly from the ruler of the state, or acts on his own responsibility. The system of government appears to suit the people, and if famines occur (and poverty generally appears to be their portion), they owe it in a measure to themselves, indolence and selfishness being their usual characteristics, although in justice to them it is only fair to mention that very little inducement is held out to cultivators to increase their holdings, the soil being considered the property of the ruler, as usual in native states; and as he claims as his due two-thirds of the crops, very little remains for the benefit of the grower. This share of the land produce, and various taxes on shawls and other manufactures, constitute the principal sources of the revenue of the country, which, large in former days, has now dwindled down to the modest sum of half a million or less per annum. The Hindu code of laws is in force in the country, and although mild, with penalties not very severe, it appears to answer the purpose. Public order is well kept; serious crimes are almost unheard of; and what strikes the visitor more particularly is the security of person and property enjoyed by all who travel in the Happy Valley, and the willing assistance and attention afforded equally by the rich and lowly among its inhabitants.

To face page 90

From a photograph by Mr H. Simpson.

Stanford's Geogl Estabt

THE THIRD CITY BRIDGE, SRINAGAR.

CHAPTER IV.

Srinagar, the Capital of Kashmir—Its Situation—The Jhelam—Srinagar the Venice of the East—Want of Cleanliness in the Inhabitants—The City Bridges—General Aspect of the City—Houses in the City—Population of the Valley—Its Inhabitants—The Kashmiris—Beauty of the Women—Character and Habits of the Kashmiris—The Hindus—The Mohammedans—The Hânjis—The Bâtal Caste—Origin of the Gipsies—Dress of the Kashmiris—Peculiar Style of dressing Hair—Language of the Kashmiris—The Literature of Kashmir—A Visit to the City—Its Public Buildings—The Boats of the Country—Climate of the Valley—Life in Srinagar—Summer Palace of the Maharajah—The Ameeri Kadal—Scene on the Banks of the River—Transmigration of the Soul of Gulab Singh—Fish and Fishing in Kashmir.

LET us next pay a visit to the capital of this fair province, now called Srinagar, or Suryea Nagar, meaning "the City of the Sun," but known by another appellation in former days. Founded about the beginning of the sixth century by the Rajah Pravarasene, the present was its first and ancient name; but being disused by the Mohammedans on their conquering the country, as savouring rather of Hindu mythology, the city was termed Kashmir, the same as the country. For several centuries it was thus known, until the advent of the Sikhs, who, Hindus themselves, restored the Hindu title, by which it is at present called.

Situated about the middle of the Valley, but close to the mountains bordering its north-western side, it is built upon both banks of the river Jhelam, extending along the shores for nearly three miles. This stream is of the utmost importance to the well-being of the city, which may be termed the Venice of the East; for it is the main artery of traffic, and, supplemented by numerous canals, forms the chief thoroughfare to any part. Streets proper do not exist, although a few dirty, narrow, roughly-paved lanes are, I believe, honoured by this appellation. Wheeled vehicles are unknown, and boats take their place, since by the medium of water communication all the affairs of life, whether of business or pleasure, are carried out. On the edges of the water are crowded the houses, and on its banks the whole population of the city seem to be always congregated, pursuing their domestic avocations or exchanging the gossip of the day. On the ghâts or steps leading down to the river are crowds of females, who appear to be perpetually engaged in filling large copper and other utensils with the element that flows at their feet, probably for culinary purposes, decidedly not for ablution; for, strange to say, this race of people, whose very doorsteps are laved by the waters of a great river, and who have never known the want of that which is so carefully utilized by the inhabitants of Hindustan, and other parts, for the necessary cleansing of the person, never apply it to any such purpose Familiarity with water must have bred contempt for one of the greatest if not the most useful of its many virtues; personal washing is unknown, and from childhood to old age they never so employ it; and instead of a people that one would expect to find the cleanliest of the cleanly, a short glance at their visible condition suffices to inform the spectator that he sees before him human beings fashioned in the image of their Creator, but, alas! for their manners and customs, veritably the dirtiest of the dirty.

The river as it flows through the city is spanned by seven bridges, which unite the two halves of the town, the Jhelam dividing it into two equal portions. All these bridges are similar in construction, and are formed of trunks of deodar driven into the bed of the stream, with quantities of stone and rock dropped around them. These form the supports for the foundations of the bridge, composed of alternate layers of stone and the trunks of Himalayan cedar-trees. On these again are laid the upper timbers of the bridge, forming the road, which in some cases is covered with a layer of earth, with the addition of a railing on either side. Such is the type of bridge met with throughout the Valley. Six others span the Jhelam in various parts beyond the city, and although rude they are strong, while the peculiarity of their construction renders them undeniably quaint and very appropriate to their general surroundings.

The general aspect of this city is extremely picturesque, the very irregularity of the rows of buildings, and the diversity of their forms, being conducive to this result. Crowded together on either bank of the river, the houses present a long line of structures varying in form, height, and material. In many wood predominates, in others stone or brick, the greater proportion being, however, a happy mixture of both. Their bases are a solid stone wall of rough masonry, those with a better built foundation owing that fact to the architect not having scrupled to avail himself of the cut stone that in former days entered into the composition of some holy Hindu temple or other ancient edifice. This foundation, affording a firm base, is raised above the level, or the probable level, of the highest floods which periodically happen in the Valley, and in many cases is of extreme antiquity, having afforded necessary support to a succession of superstructures. Above this foundation is the wood, stone, or brick building, of two, three, or more stories, and often projecting several feet over the water, being in many cases supported by props or uprights from beneath. The walls of the upper structure are usually built of brick, burnt or sun-dried, and secured in a wooden framework as a precaution against the disintegrating effects of an earthquake. Nearly all have a low, sloping roof, with extended eaves or gable ends, and they are rendered watertight by large sheets of birch bark, which is nearly impervious to moisture, laid over the rafters, while over this again is spread a mixture of finely-broken stones and earth. They all appear to have, particularly in front, facing the river, very large window spaces, beautifully finished trellis-work of diversified patterns taking the place of frames, as the thin glazed paper of the country, pasted over them from the inside, does that of glass, which appears, if not unknown, to be totally unused.

A commanding view of these buildings, which in

their irregularity afford in the sunlight such varied lights and depths of shadow, is certainly one of great beauty, and unique in character; for the style of Kashmirian architecture is decidedly peculiar to the country. Above their roofs show the mountain ridges, varying in form as one follows the turns of the river, which, alive with boats of every description, together with the stone ghâts that lead up from the water thronged with people, lends life to the scene. The unfamiliar costume too, and many other peculiarities, confirms the impression, already so evident from our surroundings, that we are in a new country, among a strange people, and one that evidently differs in many respects from the branch of the same family located on the other side of the Pir Panjál.

Of the 420,000 inhabitants of Kashmir more than a third dwell in this city and its environs, the population of Srinagar being estimated at 150,000 souls; but as no accurate census has to my knowledge been taken of late years, it is difficult to fix the number of the people dwelling either in the towns or in the Valley generally. The above figures however may be taken as about the approximate number; and what a falling off they show in the prosperity of a country which in former days reckoned its inhabitants by millions! for it is stated, although I am unable to vouch for the truth of the assertion, that at one time the number amounted to three millions. But wars, pestilence, and famine have all done their work, and are the principal causes of the depopulation of this naturally fertile spot; and even since my visit to the Valley these dire agencies have caused further decrease in the ranks of the Kashmiris; for a terrible epidemic of cholera occurred last year, followed by the inevitable scarcity, and its consequent concomitants of death and the emigration of many of the survivors.

The actual inhabitants of this country are usually styled Kashmiris, and physically are undoubtedly a fine race, the finest perhaps existing in this part of Asia, and the type of the old Aryan race, the stock from whence they have sprung. Tall, strong, and stoutly built, the features of the men are large and aquiline, with a wide, straight-up, and high forehead, a well-shaped head, and a cast of countenance somewhat like the Afghans—Jewish in character, although there is nothing known that would connect their origin with any of the tribes, lost or otherwise, of that celebrated nation.

The bulk of the inhabitants are Mohammedans, the Hindus forming only about one-seventh of the population. The two possess marked characteristics, distinguishable from each other notably as regards their complexion, which in the Mussulman Kashmiri is generally that of the olive, as found among Italians, but in the Hindus is of a fair and ruddy character, a fact they attribute to their general disuse of animal food; while the natives generally ascribe their own beauty to the peculiar softness of the water of the Valley.

The beauty of the women of Kashmir is of ancient and world-wide reputation; and certainly, as a well-known author remarks, many of them are handsome enough to induce a man to exclaim, as did the Assyrian soldiers when they beheld the beauty of Judith, "Who would despise this people that have among them such women?" As there is in this country, only excepting among the highest classes, no concealment of the features, one has a good opportunity of judging of the truth of the generally-accepted assertion as to their loveliness, which for my own part I do not consider overrated to any great degree. One certainly sees some very ugly women, both in Srinagar and in other parts of the Valley; but these are generally of a certain age, and have led a life of toil, scanty fare, and exposure. Taking them all round, among the lower classes, which, with the 'panditanis' belonging to the Brahman caste, are the ones the visitor sees the most of, the higher classes being, as elsewhere in the East, very inaccessible, they are all usually good-looking, and enough so in many cases to entitle them to be considered undeniably handsome. They are tall and well-grown; and not possessing that slimness of figure, and the marked delicacy which distinguishes the females of India, their general style rather deserves the appellation of fine than elegant. Their complexion is that of the brunette, with a good deal of pink and white on the cheek among the upper classes, which assumes a healthy brown and red in the lower, accustomed to exercise and hard work. All, however, possess a pair of large almond-shaped hazel eyes, and a set of white and regular teeth, such aids to general beauty in the female face; whilst long black eyelashes add natural brilliancy and softness to the organs of sight, and nothing is wanting to complete the picture. Despite the unbeautifying effects in many cases of poverty and misery, and the dirt which, as stated at the commencement of this chapter, generally covers them, and which has led an author and artist lately to remark that the Kashmiris reminded him of beautiful ancient statues not yet cleaned from the earth in which they had lain buried for ages, their title to beauty must justly be conceded, and a Kashmiri woman may claim one of the first places among her sex as a fine example of nature's loveliest handiwork—the female human form divine.

In character the Kashmiris have some good qualities, but these are outnumbered by their failings and faults. They are the most inveterate liars to be met with in the East, and that means a good deal in a part of the world where the inhabitants generally seem to imbibe the talent of lying with their mother's milk. They are as a race decidedly cowardly, ever ready to wrangle, but never to fight; and, if threatened by their superiors in any way, cry and act after the manner of children, consequently are not to be depended on to bear themselves well against any physical danger. They are decidedly clever and ingenious, and talkative and cheerful in disposition; but their selfishness, ignorance, and their intriguing, false, and dishonest qualities, have caused hard things to be said of them by other nations, which undoubtedly they in a measure richly deserve. My own opinion, gleaned from actual experience, decidedly suggests the idea that upon the whole the general character of the inhabitants of the Happy Valley is not an elevated one, and far from being in keeping with their poetic surroundings.

The country people do not differ much in any way from the dwellers in towns, although certainly we find in Srinagar more variety in the inhabitants, with a tendency to split up into castes, most of which are based, as in India, on the hereditary transmission of occupations. First, and distinct from all the rest, are the Hindus, who number about 38,000 in the city, most of whom are Brahmans, and to all of whom, whatever their occupation, is applied the appellation of Pundit, a title in other parts only assumed by those Brahmans learned in their theology and the expounding thereof. It is certainly curious that all the Kashmiri Hindus, the remainder of the once great and ancient nation, are of this caste, and leads one to the supposition that the greater part of the population were originally Brahman, a conclusion also indicated if we take into consideration the terms in which this country is spoken of in the early Sanskrit writers, who mention it always as a country of learned men, such as undoubtedly were originally all the members of this division of society. At the present time, however, they are not all learned men---many are writers, tailors, cloth-sellers, although a goodly number follow their ancient calling, and are an influential and favoured class. Their exertions in teaching, and their attempts to foster their ancient literature, are most praiseworthy, and in both they are aided by the head of the present dynasty, who, belonging himself, as a follower of the Sikh religion, to a sect of the Hindus, naturally rather inclines to this division of his subjects; the Hindus generally, although few in number, are undoubtedly at present the favoured class in the Vale of Kashmir.

The remainder of the inhabitants are, as already stated, Mohammedans, and the tribes and families are numerous. We have already seen how one of these families, the Chákks, or warrior class, assumed in former days regal power, but of later years they degenerated into mere banditti, and were hunted down so unmercifully that few remained. Those that were left are now known by the appellation of 'guluwans,' or 'horse-keepers,' and follow the more peaceful occupation of tending herds of cattle upon the 'margs,' or downs, where later on we will visit their homes.

There is, however, another class which deserves a few words, for they are numerous and conspicuous, and are the section of the Kashmiris with whom visitors to the Valley come most in contact. I refer to the 'hânjîs,' or boatmen; and as the river, canals, and lakes are the chief highways in the country, it naturally follows that as a body they are numerous and of some importance. They are a fine race, for both men and women have bodies well developed by the hard labour of towing and paddling the boats, which is their means of earning their living. The boats form also their homes, for the greater part of them pass their lives entirely on board, and know no other dwelling-place. They are ready and willing to act as servants to Englishmen; it is always customary to engage a number of them and a boat during one's stay in the Vale, and being active and obliging they prove of great service. They are, it is true, excessively greedy, and try by every means in their power to make as much out of their employers as they possibly can. This after all, however, one expects, for I cannot say that they are alone in this respect after my experience of India, Indian servants, and the natives of that country generally. In Kashmir, as in India, we find a class or caste whose members are outcasts from the general community. Here this is the Bâtal caste, from among whom are provided those who do the unclean work in the towns and country. They also supply the ranks of the musicians and dancing girls, whose beauty and ability to sing and dance are renowned throughout the Valley, and in the adjacent countries; but the decrease in the general prosperity of their native land has affected even their fortunes. The handsomest and most accomplished of this class are now to be found pursuing a not immaculate life at Lahore, and other towns of the Punjab, rather than at Srinagar. These Bâtals are said to be the descendants of the aboriginal inhabitants of the country before the advent of the Aryans, and there are some grounds, reasoning by the analogy of other places, for the truth of this assertion. They certainly differ from the rest of the inhabitants, who hold them in the greatest contempt, and have rather the manners and appearance of that ubiquitous tribe, the gipsy. That they are similar in many respects to the gipsies is an undoubted fact, and authors interested in this vexed subject consider it probable that the gipsies, whose religion partakes somewhat of the Buddhist form, and whose language is that of India, with many Sanskrit words intermixed, may be the descendants of Kashmiris driven from their native country in former days, by the persecutions attendant upon a change of rulers of foreign creed and tongue.

Every country has its own peculiar national costume; and the country we are treating of is not behind others in this respect, but, unlike many whose dress is becoming and picturesque, adding to the grace and dignity of the wearer, that of the inhabitants of Kashmir is decidedly the reverse; in one word, it may be called undeniably hideous. For this, however, they are not to blame. In ancient days they possessed a distinct and more appropriate costume, which was forbidden by the emperor Akbar after his conquest of the Valley, about the end of the sixteenth century, and replaced by his order by the present dress, which from that time has undergone no material change or alteration. The usual dress of the men is a pair of loose drawers, and a long, loosely-fitting shirt or smock-frock, reaching from the neck to the ankles; a turban, or more generally a skull cap; and if shoes are worn, they are either of rough, untanned hide, or of plaited grass and string. Formed of cotton for summer wear, and of woollen material for winter, in colour originally white, but from never being washed usually of a dirty brown, the dress of the men presents nothing attractive. Such as it is, it is universally worn, except by the richer classes among the Hindus, who adopt a somewhat similar costume to their brethren in Hindustan. The dress of the women is similar to that of the men—a long, loose shirt with sleeves—presenting however more diversity in colour; for it may be red, blue, or green, the first-named appearing rather the favourite hue. Their heads are covered with a small cap, usually surrounded with a fillet of red cloth; and the richer females have in addition a 'chudder' or shawl thrown over their heads and shoulders, which in most Eastern countries is employed to conceal the features from the gaze of strangers; but rarely so in Kashmir, where such a custom obtains only among those of the very highest rank. The Hindu women also wear in addition a white rolled cloth tied loosely round the waist, and, like their sisters in India, incline rather to the adornment of their persons with bangles, ear and nose rings, and other articles of jewellery. This is most marked in the case of the 'punditanis,' the wives of the pundits, perhaps the prettiest, the cleanest, and best-dressed class of the fair sex in the whole country.

One fact remains to be mentioned as regards their costume, and that is, the mode of dressing the hair, which is peculiar, and is sure to attract the attention of the stranger. It is, however, I believe, usually confined to the unmarried girls, as after entering into the holy state they are said to become rather indifferent as regards their personal appearance, a slur from which we must certainly except those of the higher classes. The hair, which with them, although rather coarse, is abundant in quantity, and usually of a glossy black colour, is drawn to the back of the head, and finely braided into a number of separate plaits. These are all gathered together, and their terminations mixed and worked up with coarse woollen thread into a large thick pigtail-like plait, to the extremity of which, for ornamentation, a long black tassel of thread is suspended.

The language of the Kashmiris is, like their dress, peculiar, and distinct from that spoken in any part of India, or of the adjacent countries. It may be considered a patois rather than a language proper, and there is a harshness and uncouthness about the pronunciation which betrays it as such. Vigne, while styling it a 'prakrit' of Sanskrit, asserts that he was told on good authority, that out of every hundred words of Kashmiri a quarter will be found to be Sanskrit, forty will be Persian, ten Arabic, and the remainder made up with Hindustani, Tibetan, and the languages of other adjacent countries. Difficult to pronounce, and difficult to acquire, it is generally incomprehensible to strangers; but that is of little account to those familiar with the dialects of India, for the inhabitants of the Valley are good linguists, most of them speaking Hindustani or Punjâbi, while many of the tradespeople and others who are thrown into contact with the European visitors speak very fair English.

From language we naturally pass on to consider literature. Little can be said on this point, for the country does not boast of much of that evidence of a nation's civilization and progress. They certainly have a few ancient works of high intrinsic value, notably the before-mentioned *Rajtaringini*, their great historical work, the *Nila Parana*, and some others, including some dramas mostly written in the Sanskrit character, although some are in the Persian. I did not see them myself, but it is stated that some of the manuscripts are written on the bark of a tree, betokening great antiquity. With these ancient efforts of literature they appear to be content; for I am not aware, although I may be wrong, of any work in their own language, nor of any of recent years in any other, attributed to a Kashmiri. From what I ascertained, I should imagine that the pundits and other learned men occupy their minds in studying that which was produced long before their time, rather than adding to the store for the benefit of the scholars of the future.

We will now pay a visit to the city, and examine more in detail the dwellings and other edifices of the Kashmiris, at which as yet we have only taken a brief and cursory glance. But few public buildings exist to attract attention, and they possess little or no architectural interest. There are, however, some ancient mosques, temples, and cemeteries that will repay the trouble of examination, and the bazaars, and shops of the various handicrafts are well worthy of a survey, for their contents in many instances are both curious and peculiar to the country. For this purpose a boat is necessary. None traverse on foot the so-called streets who can well avoid it, neither is there any necessity that they should, for the places that are likely to be honoured by our attention are all situated on the river-side, Srinagar being a city of great length, but with little breadth.

Of boats there are several varieties, according to the purpose for which they are required, and the visitor would do well to engage one with its crew for the term of his stay at this place, though, if he be not so inclined, plenty are to be hired for the day or trip at reasonable rates, as will be seen by reference to Appendix v., where these are given on an official document supplied by the Punjab government, and which in addition contains certain rules and regulations for the guidance of strangers. First we have the 'doongah,' a large long flat-bottomed boat between fifty and sixty feet in length, and nearly six in breadth; for half its length it is covered in by matting, supported on a wooden framework, with side curtains of the same material, which can be kept down or rolled up as required. This portion of the boat, utilized by the traveller, is large enough to contain a bedstead, and other articles of furniture, and is as sheltered and comfortable to reside in for a time as any tent. The hinder part of the boat is in possession of the crew, who with their wives and families make it their home, and reside in it all the year round. Both men, women, and children take part in the navigation of the vessel, which down stream is propelled by heart-shaped paddles, and drawn up stream by the united aid of the whole family harnessed like cattle to a long towing rope. There are several other large boats, such as the 'bangla,' a species of pleasure barge, and the 'baht,' used only for carrying grain, wood, or other merchandize; but they are rarely if ever used by Europeans, who on long journeys engage the first-named, with a second for their servants, and for excursions to the city, or for general use at Srinagar, one called a 'shikára,' of the same shape as the 'doongah,' but very much smaller and lighter in every respect.

The usual time for visiting the city is the afternoon; for at that period of the day the scene presented during the row down the river is at its best and liveliest, the whole population seeming to be astir, and bent on business or pleasure, although there is nothing to prevent us from sallying out at any period of the twenty-four hours, the sun not being in Kashmir the powerful enemy we seek to avoid in India. The weather in the Happy Valley, for the greater part of the year, is truly delightful, and admirably adapted to the European constitution. The climate of the lower portions is very similar to that of the South of Europe, although of course any range of temperature is obtainable by ascending higher and visiting some mountain retreat, from agreeable coolness to the cold of Norway or other northern portions of our own continent. The months of July and August are decidedly the hottest, and are particularly so felt at Srinagar, which then becomes very unhealthy. It is usual to resort to some other part to avoid this unpleasantness—Gulmarg or Sonamarg being favourite localities for this purpose, places we shall visit in company further on.

The winter season, like all the others, is pretty well marked in the Valley; and during the last month of the year, and up to the end of January, it is cold, with frost—the lakes and ponds being sometimes even frozen over. There is no actual monsoon or wet season as in India, although the surrounding mountains are subject to periodical rains, occurring about the same time as in the former country, and the fall of rain and snow in the Vale itself is by no means excessive, although frequent showers, and sometimes even heavy storms occur, very similar to those which we are accustomed to nearer home.

Nothing therefore in the weather prevents our going about at any time of the day; but, as already mentioned, the afternoon is usually selected. City life at Srinagar flows on very easily and pleasantly, if somewhat lazily; the mornings are usually taken up with eating, smoking, visiting, and gossiping with one's friends and neighbours, and bargaining with the different merchants, who daily bring to the location of the visitors, for sale, every description of article for the manufacture of which the Valley is famous.

Descending from the high path on the side of the river in front of our quarters, down rude steps cut in the bank, we step on board the 'shikára' or small boat that awaits us, and give the order to paddle down to the city. Reclining on the cushions or shawls spread at the bottom of the craft under the awning, for of seats there are none, we are comfortable enough, and as we glide gently along, are able to notice anything worth observing. The first object that strikes our attention, after passing the houses of the British Resident and other officials, is a large square building, with a verandah all round, hung with gaudy-coloured 'purdahs,' and surrounded by a stone wall, which also encloses a small garden. Situated on the left bank of the river, in the curve of a wide bend the stream makes in its course at this spot, this is a striking and picturesque object, and is in reality the abode of royalty, being the summer palace of the Maharajah, who occasionally visits it. There is nothing very remarkable about the building itself, which is of recent construction; but the rooms in the interior are curious, the walls and ceilings being formed entirely out of papier-mâché, an article for the production of which this country has long been famous. After passing this edifice the river resumes a straight course. Soon after, on the left, a ghât or landing-place is seen leading to the parade-ground, and then we come to the Ameeri Kadal, the first bridge, near which commences the well-known poplar avenue, the Rotten Row of Srinagar. Next we enter upon a wide piece of water, with either bank crowded with houses; for this is the commencement of the city proper. The scene here becomes lively enough; for boats of every description are scattered in all directions, and of the manners and customs of the inhabitants a good general idea is to be obtained; duties not performed in the open air are equally visible with those that are; for as the houses possess no windows, all that is transpiring within doors is perfectly free for our inspection. As far as one can judge, the general occupation of the great majority of the men seems to be idling about, gossiping and washing their teeth, or rather cleaning them with a piece of stick, like the natives of India, about the only personal act of cleanliness of which they seem to be guilty. The weaker sex seem to be more busily employed in washing culinary articles in the stream, exchanging at the same time, in the shrillest of voices, the gossip of the day with their friends and acquaintances. Some, however, are engaged in harder and more profitable labour, and are busily employed in grinding corn, which is done in the primitive fashion of pounding it with a thick heavy pole, the excavated hollow of a large stone serving as a mortar.

Many of the shawl and other merchants have houses overlooking the river, and about this time are to be seen busily engaged tempting our fair countrywomen with the varied products of the Kashmir loom and needle. The fishermen are also hard at work, plying their avocation; for fish forms a great proportion of the food of the poorer classes, and a famine was nearly created a short time ago by an order being issued that none were to be caught and eaten, the Maharajah having been informed that the soul of his father had entered into the body of a trout, and was swimming about near the scenes of his former triumphs. To avoid the sacrilege of destroying the blissful future of Gulab Singh, the edict went forth, that other articles of food only must be used; but as it soon appeared that its observance would be productive of much misery, it was rescinded, and the safety of the transmigrated soul of the former ruler of Kashmir left to the care of the providence that watches over such matters. There are five or six different varieties of fish in the Valley, but the most common of all is the Himalayan trout, a fish that varies so much in colour and appearance, according to age and season, that there would appear to be several species, instead of one only It rises very sluggishly at the fly, and the gentle craft would appear to be unprofitable employment, although many of the visitors pursue it with an energy worthy of a better cause. The other varieties of the finny tribe are a smaller species of trout, and some that resemble the white mullet of India; and there is also a little white fish with a bluish back, a few inches long only, which seems to be very abundant. At Sopoor, and also at other places, good 'mahseer' fishing is to be obtained, and in the capture of this noble fish—the Indian salmon—the angler forgets the poor sport afforded by the other varieties of fish in the Valley, and meets a foeman worthy of his rod and spear.

CHAPTER V.

The Embankment of the River—The Sher Garhi Fort and Palace—The Kashmirian Army—Family of the Maharajah—The Sunt-i-Kul Canal—The Kut-i-Kul Canal—The Mar Canal—The Habba Kadal—The Fati Kadal—The Shah Hamadan Musjid—Story of its Founder—The Bagh-i-Dilawur Khan—The Zaina Kadal—The Badshah—The Jumma Musjid—The Mint—Coinage of Kashmir—The New Mosque—Evidences of former Hindu Temples—The Religion of Kashmir—Naga or Snake Worship—Buddhism—Jainism—Brahmanism—Mohammedanism—Forcible Conversion of Natives of the Valley—Its effect on the Origin of the Gipsies—The Ali Kadal—The Bulbul Lankar—The Naya Kadal—The Suffa Kadal—The Eedgah—The Noor-Bagh—Office of Executioner—Termination of Trip through City.

PURSUING our course down the river—the sides of which in former days were embanked from the first to the last bridge, by an embankment composed of large blocks of limestone, of which at present the ruined remains are all that is left—we soon come to a large building, the Sher Garhi, the city fort and palace. Situated on the left bank, it presents to the river, which flows along its eastern side, a long loop-holed wall, with bastions rising between twenty and thirty feet above the general level of the water, surmounted by roomy, but lightly-built, houses. Its southern and western sides are protected by a wide ditch; the Kut-i-Kul canal bounds it on the north, and in its interior are grouped a number of dwelling-houses for the officials of the court, government offices, and barracks. On its wall, facing the river, and perched upon one of the bastions, is a large double-storied house, the abode of the Dewan or Prime Minister, and just below his residence is a long lofty building, the government treasury, containing shawls, 'pushmeena,' coin, and other valuable property. A curious-looking wooden building comes next, the Rang Mahal or 'audience hall,' a part of the royal residence, which is just below it, styled the Baradarri, and which is unquestionably the most important modern structure in Srinagar. It is a large irregular building of a peculiar style, for while partly of native architecture, one portion, with a large projecting bow, partakes somewhat of an European character. A flight of wide stone steps leads up from the water's edge at the angle of this building, and conducts into the palace. Adjoining is the temple frequented by the ruler and family, called the Maharaj-ke-Mandir, the domed roof of which is covered with thin plates of pure gold, which glitters in the sunlight, causing it to be plainly perceptible a long distance away. To reach the interior of the palace, one ascends by the before-mentioned steps, which at all times of the day appear thronged with people, some waiting to prefer petitions to the sovereign or his ministers as they descend to their boats, others to obtain a hearing or justice, which is here administered in open court daily by the governor. To the more private portion of the palace they have no access; for, guarding the gateway at the top of the stairs which leads directly into the royal abode, stands a sentry, a warrior belonging to the Kashmir army, and near by is the guard-room, what we should call in our service the main-guard.

Most of the men comprising the Kashmirian army, or rather the army of the ruler of the Kashmir and Jamoo territories, are Dogrâs, Gilghitis, and other inhabitants under his sway. The denizens of the Valley are rarely admitted into its ranks, their proverbial cowardice and timidity in any danger preventing them from making good or reliable soldiers. The artillery musters only about thirty guns, and the cavalry force is also small, the nature of the country in which they are called upon to serve forbidding their general employment. The infantry, however, make up for the deficiency; for they are probably not less than 15,000 in number, a respectable force for so small a country, but requisite, being required to garrison Ladak, Gilgit, and other portions of the Maharajah's dominions, all of which, acquired by the sword, require to be held in subjection by the same weapon. Service in the army is a pretty popular profession; for the men and the officers, who are all native gentlemen, are, I believe, well paid and well treated, and their duties are comparatively light. They appear to be well drilled and fairly dressed, both after the British fashion, which they copy to the last degree, the officers even using words of command in the English language.

The interior of the palace contains nothing very remarkable. We went over it, accompanied by the Babu, but of course were not admitted to the more private apartments. What we did see was only what is to be seen in all Eastern palaces—large halls and smaller rooms, gaudily decorated, with numerous mirrors and chandeliers of coloured glass, the only difference in this particular instance being that the walls and ceilings were made of or covered with papier mâché, painted in different patterns and devices. The eldest of the three sons of the Maharajah, the Mean Sahib, Pertab Singh, has also his residence within the walls of the palace and fort, but it needs no mention further than to remark that it is similar to his father's, on a very much smaller scale.

Immediately opposite to the palace, the Sunt-i-Kul or 'apple-tree canal' opens into the river, one of the few that traverse the interior of the city. This particular one leads to the Drogjun, or gate of the city lake, and is well worth visiting. It is navigable for boats throughout its length, showing along its winding course some fine plane and other trees on either bank, making a beautiful combination with the placid water at their feet and the rugged mountains behind them. The Kut-i-Kul canal is another watercourse on the left, just below the palace, which passes through the western portion of the city, embracing some of its most squalid parts. But the most interesting of all these watery highways is the Mar canal, perhaps the most curious place in Srinagar. It flows from the lake and intersects the northern portion of the city; and its narrowness, its walls of stone, its heavy single-arched bridges, and landing-places of the same material, joined to the gloomy passages leading down upon it, betoken the greatest antiquity, whilst the lofty but half-ruinous-looking houses on either bank seem ready to topple over down into the water. Many travellers have remarked that it bears a close resemblance to one of the old canals in Venice, and certainly, although far inferior in architectural beauty, it is very similar, and perhaps not without pretensions to equal singularity. A little further down the river we come to the Habba Kadal, the second bridge, which in former days was not unlike Old London Bridge, on a smaller scale; for a row of wooden shops ran along both its sides, overhanging the water. These were, however, all burnt down a few years back, and have never been rebuilt.

The Fati Kadal is the next bridge, and below it on the right bank is situated the Shah Hamadan Musjid, one of the most elaborate mosques in the country, and perhaps the most celebrated. Like the greater number of the mosques in Kashmir it is built of wood (usually that of the Himalayan cedar), and covered in with a projecting roof, on which at various points bells are hung; while, unlike the generality of the edifices devoted to the Mohammedan religion, a golden ball is placed on its top instead of the usual crescent. I am not certain of the date of its erection; but it is considered of great importance, and a holy shrine by the Mussulman

To face page 122

From a photograph by Mr H. Simpson

Stanfords Geog^l Estab^t

THE SHAH HAMADAN MUSJID, SRINAGAR

population, who, I understand, fully believe in the legend as regards the Shah Hamadan, its reputed founder. The story runs thus: Syud Ali, or Shah Hamadan, a true descendant of the prophet, on account of the persecutions his party endured at the hands of their king, the ruler of Samarkund, fled his country, being able, by virtue of his sanctity, to transport himself through the air to Kashmir. Having descended on the spot where the mosque now stands, he ordered the Hindu fakir, or holy man, who was there located, to depart. The fakir, who certainly possessed claims to priority of occupation, declined to do so, upon which Shah Hamadan said, That if he could bring him news from heaven, he would admit that he was a great man, and leave him in peace. This he gladly consented to do; and having numerous idols under his care, he despatched one towards heaven. Shah Hamadan, however, kicking off his slipper, struck it with such force that the image fell to the ground before much progress upwards had been made. After this feat they fell into conversation, in the course of which the fakir, stating that he was so great a man through the performance of charitable actions, was deemed by his opponent worthy of being made a convert to Islam. This was accordingly done; and his conversion was the means of the conversion of a number of Hindus, his disciples, who immediately followed his example. The fakir, assuming the name of Sheik Baba Wuli, lived afterwards in great piety, promulgating the doctrines of his new religion; and a penance of forty days performed at his shrine is considered at the present day the most meritorious act of the followers of the Prophet in the Happy Valley.

A few minutes' walk from the mosque brings us to the Bagh-i-Dilawur Khan, an old Pathan garden, once a pretty place, but now utterly neglected, although at one time it was decorated with balconied summer-houses, overhanging the waters of the lake, on the edge of which it is situated, and must have formed a charming retreat.

Below the Zaina Kadal, or fourth bridge on the same side of the river, stands a noble ruin, the Badshah, the tomb of Zinulabudin, the best ruler the Mohammedans ever gave the country, and who reigned from 1423 to 1487. The tomb is of brick, octagonal in shape, and ornamented with Saracenic arches surmounted by a single dome, surrounded by four smaller ones. It is contained within the walls of a burying-ground, which possesses numerous graves of distinguished personages in connection with the history of the country. Rather less than half a mile from this tomb stands the Jumma Musjid or 'great mosque,' a large square building of a Saracenic character, with an open square or pateo in the centre, and a wooden steeple at each angle. Built by the Emperor Shah Jehan, its foundations are of stone, but the wooden roof of the surrounding cloister, or interior, is supported by two rows of pillars, 392 in number, each being formed from a single deodar tree about thirty feet in height. It is a fine building, its interior most cathedral-like and imposing, and the ground about its exterior is interesting to the student of Kashmir history, for numerous horizontal massive tombstones betoken the last resting-place of many of the members of the powerful Chákk family, the sometime rulers over their native country.

The Mint is not far away, but is not worth the trouble of visiting. It is called the Zerab Khana, and is a small, mean, dirty-looking building. The arrangements for coining are primitive and simple enough, a piece of the metal, sufficient for one coin, being heated, beaten out on an anvil, and while hot stamped by hand with a die. In this way the Kashmir coins are made, and, as one may imagine, are rude enough in appearance. Both the silver and copper money are considerably alloyed. Of silver coinage they have three sorts of rupees in circulation—one, like the Indian variety, worth sixteen annas; one worth ten; while the smallest of the set is valued only at eight annas. The copper coins are pice—the larger equal in value to the Indian, the smaller equal to about two-thirds, both varieties being clumsy, uneven lumps of metal. All this, I believe, is soon to undergo alteration, as machinery is ordered to turn out pieces of money equal to that of a more civilized character.

There remains to be noticed another mosque—the New Musjid, or Patar Musjid, as it is often termed—which is situated on the left, the other bank of the river to that which we have been visiting, and nearly opposite the Shah Hamadan, the first edifice of the kind that engaged our attention. It is a fine structure, built of stone, having a handsome flight of steps leading from the river to the door of the court-yard that surrounds it; and its interior, of about 192 feet in length, with a proportionate breadth. contains some massive archways, the roof of the compartments between them being handsomely ribbed and vaulted.

Erected by Nur Jehan Begum; the beautiful Nurmahal, or 'Light of the Harem,' it must have been a perfect specimen of its kind, resembling somewhat in general aspect and finish the mosques at Agra. At present it appears somewhat dingy and out of repair, not having been for many years utilized for the purpose of public worship, which would have otherwise insured its protection and preservation.

It cannot fail to be noticed that most of the buildings devoted to religious observances in the city are those for the use of the followers of the Prophet. Although Kashmir has known many changes of religion, it was for many years under the sway of Mohammedans, and may, although at present under Hindu rule, be styled a Mohammedan country. With the bigotry that characterizes the followers of Islam they speedily converted their subjects to their own faith, and while erecting edifices for the practice of their own religion, their fierce zeal in many of their line caused them to destroy all those belonging to any other. This is the reason why at the present day we see hardly any vestiges of Hindu temples or other specimens of native Hindu architecture. At one time the Hindu temples in the city must have been exceedingly numerous; for, as before remarked, the foundations of many of the houses on either side of the river are very commonly formed of large blocks that have been drawn from them. A capital turned upside down, a broken shaft or pedestal, may frequently be observed doing duty for ordinary building stone, all that remains of the once massive edifices of which they formed a part, and which could never have fallen to the ground unless they had been forcibly displaced by the hand of man.

Thus very little remains as evidence of the original faith of the inhabitants of the Valley, which, early colonized by the Aryans, must have been the scene of many of the mysteries of the 'naga' or 'snake worship,' one of the earliest forms of idolatry practised at first by that race after their descent from the plains of Asia, and which appears to have taken root in Kashmir; for we find it still followed in that country long after the onward wave from the same stock had overrun parts of India, and there established the Brahmanical religion, the basis of modern Hinduism, as followed by their descendants at the present day. The isolated condition of Kashmir may have had some share in the production of this result; for we find no very reliable account of any other purer form earlier than the introduction of Buddhism by Asoka, about two centuries and a half before the Christian era. Such is the opinion of many authorities on the subject, although it is claimed by others that, according to the *Ayin-i-Akbari*, the work of Abul-Fazel, this prince abolished the Brahmanical rites, and substituted those of Jaina, an assertion which, if correct, implies that Brahmanism flourished in the country long before its supposed introduction; and also that the creed of the Jainas, which some suppose to have been the early faith of Asoka, must be added to the list of the changes in the religion of the Kashmiris.

This, however, seems to be a disputed point; for from the original text of the *Rajatarangini* it appears that Asoka by no means attempted the former of these heinous acts; and that, on the contrary, he was a pious worshipper of Siva, to whose temple he constantly repaired. His introduction of Buddhism into the Valley would also appear to be called in question; for I find it mentioned, in a work on the Jain religion, that from the evidence afforded from various sources we can only infer that Asoka's conversion to Buddhism occurred late in his life or reign. And further, that he either did not seek to spread or had not the chance or opportunity of propagating his new faith in the outlying sections of his dominions; and that in this Valley of Kashmir at least Buddhism came after him as a consequence of his southern surrender, rather than as a deliberate promulgation of a well-matured belief on his part.* Be this as it may, we possess proof, however, that this form of religion was dominant in Kashmir during the reign of his grandson and successor, Jaloka; for both the temple on the Takt-i-Suliman, and other ruined buildings at Pandritan and elsewhere, are standing evidences of the fact, which is also confirmed in the annals of the country. As to its duration, it is probable that this form of worship prevailed until some eighty years before Christ, when the Brahmanical or Hindu religion was, as is generally accepted, introduced by Abhimanyú, and became the faith of the country for several centuries after, until supplanted by that of Mohammedanism.

The introduction of Mohammedanism is generally supposed to have occurred about A.D. 1356, when, during the reign of Shahabudin, the Syud Ali Hamadan arrived in the country from Persia, attended by a great following of fugitive disciples. This fact is, however, disputed by the Kashmiris, who allege that their conversion to Islam occurred some years before this date, and was owing to the exertions of a fakir named Búlbul Shah, who,

* *Jainism; or, The Early Faith of Asoka.* By E. Thomas, F.R.S.

coming from Tibet, was the first Mohammedan that appeared in the Valley. No direct proof exists of this; but that there was such a personage admits of no doubt; for his tomb is yet standing on the right bank of the river, just below the fifth bridge. The introduction of this new religion was followed by the consequences that usually befell all countries into which its followers intruded themselves. Forcible conversion or death was the alternative presented to the inhabitants, whose only means of avoiding such a terrible choice was the abandonment of their homes to seek in other countries that toleration denied to them in their own. Many undoubtedly did so, and probably sought refuge in India, meeting, however, I should imagine, with but little better treatment; that country being about this time suffering under the invasions of the Moguls, themselves stern and bigoted Mohammedans. Others probably wandered off to adjacent parts, and it is to these bands of fugitives that it has been attempted to trace the origin of the Zingarri or gipsy tribe, it being stated in the *Life of Tamerlane* that a race of strange people, holding opinions and with manners and customs similar to those which obtain among the modern gipsies, existed at Samarkund in 1442, some few years after the time of the great persecutions in Kashmir. Those Hindus that did remain accepted their fate, and the fierce zeal of the rulers that followed leading them to destroy all vestiges attesting the existence of another creed, the country soon became thoroughly Mohammedan, both in religion and outward appearance. So it remained until its conquest by Runjit Singh, when Hinduism, or rather Sikhism, became favoured, and temples and other buildings devoted to the old religion again reared themselves in the Valley; but of the ancient examples of architecture relating to that once national creed nothing is left but ruins, or remains applied to the meanest purposes.

To continue, however, our progress down the river and through the city. Immediately below the Alli Kadal, or fifth bridge, stands an old stone building, with an inscription, supposed to be Buddhist, in the Nagri character; and some few yards below again is an evidence of another faith. This is an old wooden mosque, said to be the oldest in the Valley, called the Búlbul Lankar, containing the grave of that fakir who, as before stated, is held by the inhabitants to have been the first and prime agent in their conversion to the faith of Mohammed. The Naya Kadal, or sixth bridge, comes next, and a little further down is the Suffa Kadal, the seventh and last of the city bridges, below which, on the right bank, is a green open flat, called the 'Eedgah,' which reminds one of home, so like an English common does it appear. A fine old mosque, the Ali Musjid, stands at one extremity, shaded by some of the noblest trees in the Valley; and nearly opposite, on the left bank of the stream, is a spot of an ill-omened character, the Noor Bagh, or place of execution. In former days it was rare not to see the gallows at this place graced by some malefactor, but capital punishment is now seldom carried out; the Sikh religion discouraging the taking of human life; and the present Maharajah, a devout follower of this belief, acting so strictly up to its tenets that for many years the hangman's office has been literally a perfect sinecure, his services having never been required.

This brings us to the termination of our progress through the city, and our inspection of its principal buildings. We will now therefore retrace our steps, and before proceeding to examine the objects of interest in its environs, pay a short visit to the principal bazaars of the capital, and take a glance at the arts and manufactures for which it is famous, and the commerce of Kashmir with other countries.

CHAPTER VI.

The Bazaars of Srinagar—Natural Products of the Valley—Occurrence of Famines—Shortcomings of the Government—Cheapness of Food in Kashmir—Calculation as to Value of Land in Kashmir—The Fruits and Vegetables of Kashmir—Wine in the Valley—Growth of Hops—Trees and Flowering Plants in Kashmir—Cattle in the Valley—Sacredness of the Cow—Diet of Visitors in the Valley—The Arts and Manufactures of Kashmir—The Kashmir Shawls—Antiquity of the Shawl—Varieties of Shawls—The Kashmir Goat—Pushmeena—Manufacture of the Shawls—The Weaving—The Weavers—The Washing of the Shawls—The Jewellery of Kashmir—Papier-mâché Work—Prices of Various Articles—Trade and Commerce of Kashmir—The Dal Lake—Aquatic Plants—The Lotus—The Singhara Plant—Floating Gardens—Objects of Interest on the Lake—Hazratbal—A Moslem Relic—Fairs or Festivals—The Feast of Roses.

THERE are several bazaars or market-places in different parts of the city of Srinagar, but with one exception they are hardly worth the trouble of a visit, visitors to the capital contenting themselves with that which, situated on the right bank of the river, and about the centre of the city, contains the shops of nearly all the best workers in the different articles peculiar to the country, the shawl merchants excepted, who are to be found located in commodious houses at various parts overlooking the stream. Many of the smaller bazaars are devoted to the sale of the necessaries of life, and if curious in this respect, the stranger will, if he pays a visit to one of them, get a good insight into the productive capabilities of the Valley and the articles of food utilized by its inhabitants. Of these there are a great variety; for nature is in general very bountiful in Kashmir, both on land and water, although at times, like its near neighbour Hindustan, the crops fail, owing to drought or other causes, and famine stalks in hideous nakedness throughout the land. Such is the case, I regret to say, at the present time, fears being even entertained that unless speedy succour arrives almost the total depopulation of the Valley will ensue.* But such help as we were able to afford to our suffering fellow-creatures in India, during the recent times of scarcity, is not so easily rendered in this part of the world, particularly at the present time; for no great store of grain exists in adjacent countries, and even if it did, the difficulties of the transport of any

* Alarming accounts of the state of the country are now being received; since the above was written, and as these pages are passing through the press.

considerable quantity are almost insurmountable. That the government of Kashmir are to blame for their supineness and carelessness in not providing against such an eventuality admits of no doubt; but then it must be remembered that this dread calamity is taking place in the East, among a people who rarely think of the future. 'Sufficient for the day' is their motto; and their very religion, or that of the greater number of them, teaches and inculcates the dogma, that all and every calamity, even if it can be obviated with very little exertion, is fate and the will of God, and that they must bear themselves resignedly under the circumstances, and hope for better days to come. That better days are not far distant I am sure we all most devoutly wish, for the depopulation and ruin of this once fertile spot would be a great calamity. However, I will not dwell upon this, but proceed to describe the Valley as I saw it, to which condition, under the blessing of Providence, I hope it may again shortly attain.

At the time of my visit to the country food for the natives was, as is usually the case there, both cheap and abundant, the prices of many articles creating, not only a feeling of astonishment to myself and companion, but also to our usually apathetic Indian servants. The chief article of consumption with the Kashmiris appears, as in some parts of India, to be rice; but wheat, barley, maize, and other seed crops are likewise cultivated. Rice is, however, the staple grain of Kashmir, the principal sustenance of its population, and a great article of revenue; the wealth even of an estate or parcel of land being calculated, not by its money value, but by the number of measures of rice it can produce. Of vegetables and fruit there are any quantity, retailed at prices that would astonish the vendors of Covent Garden. Cabbages, turnips, cucumbers, lettuces, and various other esculents, are very abundant, and are extensively used. But it is the fruit of the Valley that most astonishes strangers; for the soil, a very rich and fertile alluvium, aided by a moist atmosphere and genial temperature, yields wonderful crops of walnuts, mulberries, peaches, cherries, pomegranates, nuts, apples, quinces, pears, and grapes. Most of these grow in our own island, but must be highly cultivated to attain to any perfection; whereas in Kashmir nature alone seems to be the gardener, for many of the flats of ground on which the trees and vines flourish appear to be totally uncultivated and uncared for. Of grapes there are, it is said, some eighteen varieties, and they may be bought at the rate of several pounds for an anna, rather less than three halfpence. The peaches, which are very fine, and with a better flavour than our hot-house sorts, can usually be procured at the rate of a dozen or so for the same money. Wine was at one time made from the grapes of the Valley, and a large number of immense ancient jars have been dug up at various times. These are supposed to have been the receptacles for the generous fluid, buried for its preservation, as I believe is the case in some Eastern countries at the present day. During the Pathan regime wine was again made, after a total cessation of its manufacture for many years; but the attempt was not successful, and it has now been entirely given up. So also has the production of cider, from the great quantity of apples yearly grown all over the country, which undoubtedly would produce a beverage equal to the very best Devonshire, if under proper management. The climate is not warm enough to allow the sugar-cane to thrive; but cotton of good quality can be produced, the fields for its cultivation being usually upon the tops of the 'kareewahs,' as it does not require the irrigation necessary for most of the other crops.

The cultivation of hops has lately been attempted on a small scale, and I should imagine would prove remunerative, as all that could be grown might be taken by our breweries in India. One of the largest of these rival establishments to Burton-on-Trent is at Marri, and brews beer that leaves nothing to be desired. Meeting the enterprising manager of the company during our visit to Kashmir, I am able to assert on his authority that the hops grown here are of good quality, and that he was then seeking to obtain a grant of land for the cultivation of the plant on a larger scale.

Of trees and shrubs I will say but little. There are several varieties of firs on the surrounding mountains. The deodar or Himalayan cedar is very abundant, and its wood is largely employed in many useful purposes. The plane or chenar tree, and the poplar, willow, and many others, grow abundantly, although the first-named is not indigenous, but was introduced by the governor, Ali Mardan Khan, who ruled in Kashmir under the Moguls in 1642. Once introduced into the country, the plane trees appear to have thriven to a wonderful degree; for they are the noblest trees in the Valley, and are everywhere to be seen, affording at the present day as grateful a shade to the inhabitants of the villages and farm-houses, as they yielded in days long past to the royal denizens of the now ruined palaces they still guard and shelter. Shrubs and flowering plants as well as ferns abound in certain localities, and several varieties used in medicine, such as aloes, chiretta, rhubarb, wormwood, &c., grow wild and in luxuriant profusion. Saffron is also largely cultivated; but we shall visit its glowing beds in their home at Pampoor. Enough has now been said, without wearying the reader, concerning the vegetation and cultivation of Kashmir, to convince anyone that in its day of prosperity, if abundance and variety of nature's free gifts can be taken into account, it fully deserves the appellation that has been given to it so often in these pages, of the smiling, fertile, and Happy Valley.

As various sorts of grain, vegetables, and fruit form the chief articles of diet of the inhabitants, cattle-farming on a large scale is not entertained; for with the exception of the richer classes of Mohammedans, who eat the flesh of sheep and goats, the majority require little but the natural productions of the soil.

The domestic animals found in the Valley resemble those of adjacent countries. The horses, cows, and oxen, are small, but the sheep are of a fair size, and are pretty numerous, if price is any criterion, as they may be purchased for one to four rupees each. The cow being held by the Sikhs as a very sacred animal is never killed, and beef is unknown alike to the Kashmiris and, during their stay, to the visitors, who must perforce content themselves with mutton, supplemented by fowls and ducks, which are very abundant, costing only about an anna a bird to purchase. Milk, however, can be purchased, with eggs and fish; and as almost all the farmers are supplied with honey, bees being kept in the walls of the farm-houses, any amount of this delicacy is obtainable. Take it altogether, therefore, one is able to fare plentifully if not sumptuously in Kashmir at very little expense, and if luxuries for the table are required, the Parsee shopkeepers at Srinagar will be most happy to supply them, and a very long bill for the same into the bargain.

Our attention is now claimed by the arts and manufactures of the country, good specimens of which are to be seen and purchased in the different shops in the big bazaar already spoken of on the right bank of the river. In weaving, embroidering, and working in metals, the Kashmiris have a great reputation; but they are also very expert in the manufacture of wooden articles, such as toys and turnery; ornamental carving; inlaid work in wood, ivory, mother-of-pearl, papier-mâché; jewellery, leather, paper, and attar of roses. It is however for the manufacture of the famous Kashmir shawls that they are best known, since these are of world-wide reputation. And although at the present time the decrees of fashion have almost banished them from Europe, and the admirable imitations produced in France, and Paisley in Scotland, exercise a great influence over the trade, yet a goodly number are still woven annually in the country of their birth, the demand for them in the East being maintained as necessary appendages to rank and state. It is a well-known fact, that the article of dress called a shawl is perhaps of higher antiquity than any other garment; but of its manufacture in these early days we possess but little information until we come to the time of Akbar, about the year 1556, when the celebrated Kashmir shawls were amongst the most important manufactures of the world, and were thought worthy of being minutely described in the *Ayin-i-Akbari*, or the *Institutes of the Emperor*, so frequently mentioned in the preceding pages. Thus Kashmir, if it cannot claim the honour of being the country of the birth of their manufacture, may undoubtedly claim that of being the country where the industry was first carefully fostered and encouraged, and whence it spread over the greater part of India, and to other more remote parts of the civilized world.

In the *Ayin-i-Akbari* mention is made of four distinct classes of shawls. First come those of remarkable lightness and softness, usually self-coloured, and made from wool undyed. The second variety were woven of wool in the natural colours—white, black, or grey, and were probably of plaid patterns, like the shepherd's plaid in Scotland. The third were called gold-leaved, probably from being embroidered with that material. The fourth were long pieces, used to enwrap the whole body, or to fashion into divers articles of attire.

These productions of the Kashmirian loom, which still remains of old and unimproved construction, are yet made in the Valley, as in the days of Akbar; but in addition to shawls, gloves and socks, red silk cloth, cotton rugs, and 'patto,' a coarse kind of cloth, and a finer variety made from camel's hair, are manufactured. These, however, need no further description, the shawls proper being more particularly our present subject. All shawls are made from what is termed 'pushmeena,' which is the short undercoat or fleece of the Kashmir goat, a variety of that animal remarkable for very long, fine, and silky hair; but whose appellation is evidently a misnomer, since it is not so generally found in the country whence it derives its name as in Western Tibet, where immense herds are reared upon the mountains. The under fleece, called 'pushm,' is a cotton-like down which grows close to the skin, beneath the usual coating of hair, and is evidently a provision of nature against the effects of the intense cold experienced in these inhospitable regions; for it does not exist on the same or any other animal in warmer latitudes. Each goat possesses but little 'pushm,' a single one not yielding more than three ounces, which is of a white colour if the animal be white, and dun-coloured if it be black or any other shade. Brought down from Ladak, *viâ* Leh, the white variety is sold in Kashmir at four or five rupees a 'seer,' or two pounds, the coloured sort being somewhat cheaper; and it is then cleaned and spun into thread, which is dyed of different colours. Some, however, is retained undyed, for the weaving of shawls of a natural shade. After the thread is dyed, it is dipped into rice-water to make it stronger, and fit it to be more safely moved by the shuttle, the stiffness being afterwards removed by washing. The shawls are woven in pairs, in very rudely-constructed looms. The weaving takes some considerable time—more than a year being occupied by three or four hands in producing a pair of good size and quality. They are woven in many pieces, being afterwards joined together with great artistic skill. The pattern is worked in with wooden needles, a separate needle being required for each colour. There are a great variety of patterns worked on the various shawls, and on their borders; but the one with which we are most familiar, and which appears to be the favourite, is the well-known 'pine,' or Kashmir pattern, and the 'fool's-cap,' or cypress-shaped ornament.

The curves made by the windings of the river Jhelam before it enters the city are said to have afforded the idea of the first-named pattern, and the second is an imitation of the aigrette of jewels worn on the turban by every great man in the East. The manufacture of shawls being under government control, a duty is imposed on every pair made; heavy penalties being also inflicted if a genuine article is not produced. The manufacture is carried on in the city, in single houses, or in factories, and the weavers, or 'wabster bodies,' as they would be termed at Paisley, are easily distinguishable from the mass of the population by their stunted frame and sickly look, the usual characteristics of those that follow this occupation in every other part of the world.

But it is not only in Srinagar that this industry is pursued, for many of the farmers and their families occupy their spare time in weaving; and I well remember our astonishment, when taking refuge from a storm at a farm-house, many miles out in the country, to find ourselves, on opening a door which presumedly led to the cow-house or stables, in a room dirty and close enough to poison a dog, but the atmosphere of which was evidently of indifference to the family of our host, who were all, from the aged grandsire down to the youngest-born, busily employed at a roughly-made loom in weaving a pair of shawls, which were estimated to be of the value of 3,000 rupees each. The worthy agriculturist told us further that they would not be completed under three years, but that the price would amply repay him. This it certainly would, even if he got considerably less than he stated, the most expert of weavers rarely earning more than a small rupee a day, but which, so far as the expenses of living are concerned, is fully equal to ten shillings per diem in England. After being taken from the loom and stamped, it becomes necessary to wash the shawls to get rid of the stiffness of the rice starch remaining in the thread, as well as generally to soften them. According to Vigne (and as bearing on the subject of what is considered to be of great importance in the manufacture, it is well worth quoting*), the best water for this use is found in the canal between the lake and the flood-gates at the Drogjun. Some ruins, in large lime-stone blocks, are lying on the washing-place, and in one of these is a round hole about a foot and a half in diameter, and a foot in depth. In this the shawl is placed, and water being poured over it, it is stamped on by naked feet for about five minutes, and then taken into the canal by a man standing in the water; one end is gathered up in his hand, and the shawl swung round and beaten with great force upon a flat stone, being dipped into the canal between every three or four strokes. This occupies about five minutes. The shawls are then dried in the shade, as the hot sun spoils the colours, and in ten days afterwards the coloured shawls undergo a similar process, but occupying less time. The white ones, after being submitted to the process, on the first day are spread in the sun, and bleached by water sprinkled over them. They then are again

* *Travels in Kashmir*, pp. 129, vol. ii.

treated by the same process as the coloured shawls, being stamped upon, and beaten a second time, and then bleached again till they are dry, and then for a third time beaten, stamped upon, and finally sun-dried. In the second time of stamping soap is sometimes used, but is not good generally, and is never employed for the coloured shawls, as the alkali might affect the hues. There is something in the water of the canal which certainly communicates to the shawls a softness which cannot be given to those manufactured at any place in the plains of Hindustan. At the same time those made in Paris or elsewhere would be probably as soft, were it not for the greater closeness of the texture, consequent upon their being made by a machine instead of the hand. For the same reason it is well known that the calico made in India is much softer, and much more durable than that made in England.

Such, then, is a brief outline sketch of a manufacture for which this country is renowned, and which in recent times has passed through many vicissitudes. In the beginning even of this century there were thousands of looms at work, replaced now by hundreds, and a great number of these beautiful fabrics were imported into Great Britain and the continent of Europe, a branch of trade now of very little value. But fashion may change, and for the future and prosperity of Kashmir it is to be hoped it will. The art is not lost; it is not dead, but in abeyance only; and there are a number of cunning hands now unemployed ready and willing to turn out as perfect specimens as ever of those Kashmir shawls, without which a few years ago no fashionable lady deemed her wardrobe complete.

The Kashmiris are, as before stated, very ingenious workers in metal, manufacturing good weapons, such as guns and swords and other articles. But their jewellery specially demands attention, the gold and silversmiths of Srinagar being very clever at their trade, producing admirable work, great quantities of which are now finding their way to England. In gold they fashion the usual articles of jewellery as seen at home; but it is in the silver articles they display more of what may be termed native taste, all their trays, goblets, jugs, tea-cups, scent-holders, being chased or engraved in divers patterns, more commonly the well-known shawl one, while some are parcel gilt, giving them a peculiar and strikingly Oriental appearance. The gold they use should be pure, and their silver should only contain sufficient alloy to render it workable; but of this, in the fulfilment of any order, you possess no guarantee, even if you had the materials worked up under your own eye. For they are, like their brethren in India, cute and cunning imposters, and, imperceptibly to the onlookers, are in the habit of concealing in the mouth particles of baser metals, which they pass down the blow-pipe they are using, for incorporation into that which is subsequently sold to you as being of virgin purity. All the articles manufactured in silver are likewise produced of similar patterns in pure copper, which after arrival home can be electro-plated; and so perfectly do such take the gilding that, with the exception of their weight, it is impossible to distinguish them from articles of richer metal.

Another interesting art is their manufacture of papier-mâché, or some similar composition. The painting on articles of this material is both curious and elegant. This is not done with oil colours, but the flowers and other ornaments are raised or modelled on the surface by means of a composition paste, then painted and oiled several times, and rubbed with the hand until they have the appearance of being varnished. In this material they commonly make such matters as boxes, waiters, cigar-cases, &c.; but larger things, such as tables, chairs, bedsteads, are also manufactured, and are used by the princes, the nobility, and the wealthy ones of the land.

Such are the chief manufactures for which the Kashmiris are famous, and very few visit the Valley without purchasing and bringing away some specimens. Regarding the price of each no fixed tariff exists, except perhaps in the case of gold and silver work, when the ordinary rate for working is two annas for every British rupee weight, if a simple pattern, and double that amount if more elaborate, in addition to the value of the metal employed. In purchasing the various other articles, the same process has to be gone over as in other parts of the East, where the buying of anything resolves itself into a species of duel between purchaser and vendor, four times as much, or even more, being asked than is ultimately taken, if one's patience and power of argument holds out long enough to conduce to such a happy result. In buying shawls or other articles of a similar sort, examine them all over carefully, and at different times of the day, for as a rule no shawl-vendor can be induced to display his stores until the approach of evening, being well aware of the superior brilliancy imparted to their tints by the slanting rays of the setting sun.

As to the commerce of Kashmir with other

countries, little can be said. That there is some amount of traffic carried on between it and the Punjab is certain, Kashmir exchanging its native productions for such things as English piece-goods, cotton, tea, sugar, porcelain, copper, tin, and dye-stuffs, and other articles foreign to the country. Great hopes were entertained a few years back of largely increasing the amount of trade that has been for some time carried on between Eastern Turkestan and India, through Kashmir, much to the advantage of that country. But despite a mission sent by our Government to that part of Central Asia, and commercial treaties with the Maharajah, I have not heard of any great results, although when I was in the Punjab the traders there were very enthusiastic over the matter, and a company was being formed to develop the traffic.

Having now pretty well exhausted the sights of the city, we will take a glance at the objects of interest to be found in its environs, chief among which is the Dal, or city lake, the chief scene of the localities immortalized by Moore in *Lalla Rookh*, and around which are to be found some of the most attractive spots of the whole neighbourhood. This lake, which is situated on the north-eastern side of the city, measures about five miles from north to south, and two miles from west to east, and is shallow in some parts, deep in others, with water everywhere of the very clearest description. On three of its sides it has a background of a mountainous amphitheatre rising to a great height above the water; and on the ground at the base of these mountains nestle, half hid by fruitful orchards, numerous small villages, and, testifying to its former celebrity, the remains of the several renowned gardens and summer palaces constructed by the different Delhi emperors. The lake may be reached by the Sunt-i-Kul canal, which connects it with the Jhelam, entering the river, as before mentioned, just opposite to the Sher Garhi, or fort and palace. But the best way to proceed, especially for those who leave the English quarter or encampment for the purpose, is to walk to the Drogjun or water-gate of the Dal, and have a boat ready on the lake at that spot to meet you. The lake here is narrow, being rather indeed a branch than the Dal itself, and appears at first to be a stagnant river or canal, covered with rushes, lotus, and singhara plants, through the green mass of which several channels pass. Taking the one leading northward, we proceed on our way, and at first cannot fail to be struck with the immense wealth of aquatic plants that surrounds us on every side, the most striking of all, especially when in flower, being the lordly lotus.

The lotus (*Nelumbium speciosum*) is very common, both on this lake and on every other similar expanse of water in Kashmir; in fact the leaves are so numerous that in some places they form a veritable green carpet, over which numerous aquatic birds, as ducks and moor-hens, run securely to and fro. When in blossom, such places present a beautiful sight. Lilies of various colours peep from amidst the verdant covering, the leaves forming which rest lightly and gracefully on the water; while the queen of all this species, the magnificent lotus, with its gigantic leaf and tall and quivering stem, drooping under the weight of the exquisite and noble tulip-shaped pink and white flower, appears in the midst of this floating garden like a reigning beauty, bowing with modest yet dignified grace, at the homage and admiration of her gaily-bedecked but less favoured rivals. Numerous other plants are to be found on the lake, as well as several varieties of reeds and rushes, of which matting is made. The 'singhara' or horned water-nut, too, is in places very abundant, and is a source of a considerable amount of revenue to the government.

It is considered State property, and the nuts are gathered annually and sold to the people. Ground into flour, and made into bread, it forms a principal article of diet to many, particularly to the boatmen and the dwellers on the margin of the lakes. The root of the lotus is also collected, and, under the name of nadru, is sold in long cylindrical pieces. When boiled and flavoured it is said to be good and highly nutritious, and is much esteemed by the inhabitants of the Valley.

The boat makes but slow progress down the narrow channel, affording plenty of time to admire the luxuriant vegetation around; but soon we have something else to interest us, for on the left bank of the lake stands the little village of Budmarg, near which almost all the shawls manufactured in the Valley are washed in the manner described a few pages back. Another small village is a little further on, and beyond this is the picturesque and elegant stone bridge of three Saracenic arches, built by one of the Moguls. Commencing on the right of this bridge, usually termed the 'Naiwidyar,' is the 'Sutoo,' an artificial causeway extending completely across the lake. About a mile beyond the bridge, we come to a portion of the lake almost covered by the celebrated floating gardens of Kashmir, which, however, at the present day do not grow flowers, but the more humble melons, cucumbers, and other vegetables.

The gardens are formed in the following manner:* The roots of aquatic plants growing in shallow water are divided about two feet under the water, so that they completely lose all connection with the bottom of the lake, but retain their former situation in respect to each other. When thus detached from the soil, they are pressed into somewhat closer contact, and formed into beds of about two yards in breadth, and of an indefinite length.

The heads of the sedges, reeds, and other plants of the float are now cut off and laid upon its surface, and covered with a thin coat of mud, which, at first intercepted in its descent, gradually sinks into the mass of matted roots. The bed floats, but is kept in its place by a stake of willow driven through it at each end, which admits of its rising and falling in accommodation to the rise or fall of the water.

Soon after passing through the multitude of these aquatic beds we enter upon the open water of the lake, and take in at a glance its beauty and its surroundings, the most delightful and interesting places to visit on it being undoubtedly the Garden of Bliss,

* MOORCROFT, vol. ii. p. 137.

the Isle of Chenars, the Nishat Bagh, and the far-famed Shálimar.

Before taking these in detail, however, let us conclude this chapter by a short visit to Hazratbal, a large village on the western side of the lake, and a place of pilgrimage to all devout Mohammedans. This place is famous for its mosque, which possesses, in a small box with a glass lid, a venerated relic, no less than a veritable or supposed veritable, hair of the Prophet's beard, which constitutes this place one of their most sacred shrines or 'zearats,' of which they possess several in various parts of the Valley. On every fête-day this relic is exhibited to the people, the Mohammedans regarding it with awe and veneration; the Sikhs, Hindus, and others—for Kashmiris of all ranks, kinds, and ages are there—with curiosity; while all unite, after this act of devotion has been duly paid, in holding a sort of carnival or feast for the rest of the day, in fact a perfect fair, which is very picturesque and well worth seeing.

There are several great fairs or festivals held yearly in Kashmir. A very large one takes place about the beginning of August on the lake, while the one that has been poetically termed 'the feast of roses' is also held on the same spot.

This is in May, when trees and rose-bushes are in full bloom; but very little poetry is observed now in its maintenance, rough play and vulgar eating and drinking taking the place of the romantic scenes when,

> "All love and light,
> Visions by day, and feasts by night!
> A happier smile illumes each brow,
> With quicker spread each heart uncloses,
> And all is ecstasy; for now
> The Valley holds its Feast of Roses."

CHAPTER VII.

The Garden of Bliss—The Silver Island—The Golden Island—The Nishat Bagh—The Shálimar Garden—Invitation to a Fête—Launch of a Steamboat—Memorable Day in the History of Kashmir—Excitement of the Inhabitants of the Valley—Scene on the Lake—The Launch—A Mishap—Proceed to the Shálimar Garden—The Illumination of the Shálimar—Its Effect—A Nautch—The Dinner—Return to our Quarters—The Harri Parbat Fort—The Great and Small Parade Grounds—The Gun Factory—The Ram Bagh—The Game of Polo—Antiquity of the Game—Prevalence of the Game in Baltistân—A Game of Polo at Srinagar—The Play—Concluding Ceremonies of the Game.

THE Nasseeb Bagh, or 'Garden of Bliss,' is situated a short distance only from the village and mosque honoured by the possession of the capillary treasure, and is a cool and pleasant spot. Its name implies as much; and it has or used to possess another, which signified, I understand, 'the garden of delicious breezes.' In the days of its prosperity, during the time of Akbar, who laid it out, and of his successors, it was evidently a garden whose chief feature was a noble grove of chenars. Many of these, in very fine condition, remain; but many are wanting, the few that still rear their lofty heads being, with the exception of some ruined masonry, all that is left of this abode of bliss.

Opposite to this garden, and in the centre of the northern portion of the lake, is the artificially-formed island, the Char Chenar, Rupa Lank, or 'Silver Island.' Its formation is stated to have been the idea of Nur Begum, the wife of Jehangir, who carried it into effect by causing a mass of masonry to be built up and covered with earth, forming a small garden of about an acre in extent, ornamented at each corner by a single chenar tree, whence its name, the Isle of Chenars. A companion to this isle exists in the Sona Lank, or 'Golden Island,' situated in the middle of the southern or other portion of the lake, very similar in construction, although somewhat larger, more verdant, and with the ruins of a building in its centre.

The Nishat Bagh is a fine old pleasure-garden, said to have been built by the Emperor Jehangir, and lies on the ground at the foot of the mountains that bound the eastern margin of the lake. It consists of a large walled enclosure, reaching from the water's edge to the rising slope of the hillside, and is arranged in terraces to suit the fall of the ground.

To face page 161

From a photograph by Mr. H. Simpson. Stanford's Geogl. Estabt.

THE MARBLE PAVILION, SHALIMAR GARDENS.

A line of tanks runs through its entire length, with strips of ground arranged as flower-beds or grass paths on either side; while fountains innumerable, and cascades formed by inclined walls of masonry, make a pretty sight when in full play; the water for this purpose being derived from a small stream that runs down from the mountains.

The Shálimar Bagh, from Shah-il-imirat, 'royal gardens,' is perhaps the most interesting place on the lake; for it was the best loved abode of the Great Moguls when visiting the Valley, and under its roof many a pleasant day was spent by the Shah Jehan and his wife, the fair lady of the Taj at Agra: are not its glories most glowingly described in the pages of *Lalla Rookh?* Built by the Emperor Jehangir, the Shálimar itself is a building placed at the upper end of a large garden, walled in, and fully half a mile long, and nearly a quarter of a mile broad. This garden is connected with the lake by a wide canal, on whose sides are broad paths extending for nearly a mile before entering the Shálimar gardens proper, through which it is continued, or rather joined, on a smaller scale beyond in the shape of a line of tanks or reservoirs leading down in cascades and level runs alternately, connected by a watercourse of varying width. This with the tanks is lined with polished limestone and crowded with fountains. The tanks and watercourse lead down the middle of the length of the garden, which is arranged in four low terraces of nearly equal size. On each side of the canal and tanks is a broad causeway or walk, overshadowed by chenar and other trees, with a few smaller walks branching off into the shrubberies—at the present day nothing but a wild and ragged undergrowth. On the uppermost or fourth terrace stands the building, a magnificent pavilion of polished black marble, raised upon a platform in the centre of a square reservoir, which contains in its circumference one hundred and forty fountains, and is filled by the water of a stream issuing from the mountains that tower behind the garden. The roof of the pavilion, which is open, is flat, and supported on each side by a range of six pillars of the same material as the rest of the building. On two of its sides there is an open corridor, and in the centre a passage, right and left of which are two rooms, the private apartments of the royal family being built against the boundary wall on either side of the terrace on which the pavilion stands.

This was used not so much as a place of abode, but as a banqueting-hall, a favourite place for entertainments of various kinds. And for this purpose it was well suited; and when at night the fountains were playing, and the canal and its cascades, the pavilions and garden, were lit up with various coloured lamps, shedding their light upon the throng of gaudily and jewel-bedecked guests, the effect must have been beautiful indeed in those days of pomp and show. In a minor degree we were so fortunate as to see it in its greatest perfection, even if shorn of some of its former elegance, as we were bidden to a fête within its walls, given by the Maharajah in honour of the launching of a small steam-vessel upon the lake.

This event, and the subsequent festivities at the Shálimar, were very diverting to us, and, by way of concluding the description of the Dal lake, a short sketch of that memorable day in the history of Kashmir may very well here find a place. A memorable day indeed it was to the inhabitants of the Valley, and long talked of both before and after; for steam power was a mystery to them, and never before had the mountains surrounding their homes echoed back the sound of the whistle, the shrill scream of that invention which proves wherever it is introduced the most civilizing agent, and the most potent uprooter of old ideas and prejudices known to man. At an early hour of the day which was to mark the first step of the onward march of progress in Kashmir, the city was full of people, and the river crowded with boats of every size and description. The entire population of the Valley were gathered together, all thrilling with excitement, and all actuated by the same motive, that of getting as good a place as possible near the scene of action, so as to obtain a sight of that mystery of mysteries, a boat moving over the water without the usual, and to them well known, agency of hands. Their first introduction to this new and unknown motive-power being made in connection with a boat—one of the institutions of the country, and with the working of which all were familiar—undoubtedly explained the great interest taken in the proceedings by both young and old; for I question if the first essay had been a piece of machinery applied to any other purpose half the curiosity manifested would have been aroused. But to move a boat was intelligible enough, although the means employed were incomprehensible; and already hopes were aroused and visions were opened of the day when the weary work of towing and paddling should be a thing of the past, and their floating homes should walk the waters, like things of life, without any exertion on their part.

If applied to the vessel they were about to see, why should it not be applied to all and sundry? Full of these hopes and aspirations, and bursting with curiosity, the people all wended their way, hours before the time fixed for the ceremony, to that portion of the lake devoted to its performance, and soon the capital presented a deserted and forlorn appearance.

The hour fixed for the important ceremony was four o'clock; and arriving on the scene about that hour, we found ourselves in a mass of boats, all wedged closely together and ranged in a double line, so as to keep a space of clear water in the centre for the steamer to proceed on her triumphal way. On the bank of the lake at one extremity of this space a grand stand had been erected, which was occupied by the Maharajah, his court, and the majority of the strangers then visiting the Valley. Soldiers stood all around, and the royal musicians were discoursing the music of their native land, which, lacking sweetness or even harmony, was yet loud enough to satisfy the Oriental taste, and add to the noise and uproar incidental to any show in the East. Directly in front of the stand and resting lightly on the water was the innocent cause of all this excitement; for it was not so much a launch as a trial-trip we were to witness, the vessel having been put together and committed to its proper element some time before. The boat itself was one of the steam-launches usually carried by the ships of the Royal Navy, and was a present to the Maharajah from our gracious Queen, having been sent to his country in pieces, which were finally put together, under the direction of a European engineer who accompanied the gift, and who remained in charge to instruct the recipient and his attendants as to the management of the machinery. Very soon after our arrival the occupants of the boats that surrounded us, for we did not attempt to land or make our way to the place of honour, became if possible more excited than ever, and shrieked, gesticulated, and swayed about on their frail crafts, each laden with human beings to the utmost extent of its carrying power, and we knew the crisis was at hand. The Maharajah took his seat on the deck in a solemn and dignified manner, but having withal an anxious appearance, as if not quite certain what was going to happen. Probably he had been told that steam, like fire, is a good servant but a bad master, and that boilers sometimes burst, and accidents will happen, despite every reasonable precaution. This may have had some effect, as he was that day brought into personal contact with the power of steam for the first time, for he looked grave; but with the courage worthy of his regal descent he took his seat, and gave the word to start. The whistle sounded, the musicians blew their loudest, the drummers smote their drums until their arms ached, and the people shouted so that the mountains echoed back the sound. Yet with all this the old adage of 'man proposes' was exemplified, for the vessel would not move. We observed much running to and fro on the part of the engineer and his assistants, and our ears were assailed with loud and discordant shrieks from the steam whistle and escape-pipe; but it was all of no avail, the vessel stirred not. We waited some time, but not finding our patience in any way rewarded, pushed our way without the heaving mass, and rowed straight across the lake to the Shálimar Gardens, where the second part of the entertainment, the feasting, was to take place. We were almost the first to start, but the remainder of the guests were not long in following our example; while the bulk of the Kashmiris, hovered about the scene for some considerable time in hopes of witnessing something remarkable. Their hopes were not, however, then fulfilled; for it was not until the following day that the defect in the machinery which caused the failure in the proceedings was rectified That having been done, the boat was brought through the canal from the lake on to the river Jhelam, when its acquisition proved a source of great amusement to the Maharajah, who every evening steamed up and down the watery highway of the city, looking as pleased as a child with a new toy, much to the delight of his faithful subjects, who clustered like bees on every commanding point that afforded a view of the royal progress.

When we arrived at the canal that led from the lake to the entrance of the Shálimar it was quite dark, but on gaining the garden a blaze of light burst on our view; myriads of lamps illuminated the whole place, causing the jets from the countless fountains to fall apparently in showers of flame. By the side of the walks on each side of the canal that runs through the centre of the garden were stationed soldiers, motionless and erect, about a yard apart, each holding in his right hand a blazing torch. The entire structure of the pavilion at its upper end, and the surrounding garden, was literally bathed in light, the tanks and watercourses appearing like fiery lakes, and when viewed from below the nature of the ground and the terraced form in which it was laid out added much to its beauty. This was, however, seen at its best from the uppermost terrace, upon which the pavilion stood. From this elevated standpoint we could take in the whole scene, and observe the lines of fire descending in regular gradation, tier after tier, until lost in the calm, dark waters of the lake, and, standing in this hall of a thousand lights, could picture to ourselves—

> "That evening (trusting that his soul
> Might be from haunting love released
> By mirth, by music, and the bowl)
> The imperial Selim held a feast
> In his magnificent Shálimar."

It was truly a lovely spectacle, and the numerous servants and soldiers of the prince, in their gay and fanciful costumes, added to its charm. Imagination was carried back to the days of childhood. The fairy-tales one had read at that time appeared to be realized, and the elfin land of our dreams, so often pictured in our thoughts, stood revealed at last. Dinner for the European visitors was laid out in the large hall, but before its welcome announcement we all stood patiently in another room, awaiting the arrival of our royal host, who soon appeared, with a large surrounding of officers of state and courtiers.

Taking his seat, the signal was given for the commencement of the inevitable nautch, without which no Eastern fête would be complete. This infliction we bore silently and resignedly; for an infliction it is to Europeans, although all Eastern people appear to take huge delight in the performance. The dance in Kashmir did not appear to differ in any way from the Indian nautch, familiar to all of us then present. The girls, who were pretty, were clothed, or rather wrapped up, in the countless folds of muslin affected by the sisterhood, and the posturing and waving of arms, and accompanying music, were identical with those of nautches elsewhere; and we all felt relieved when the final shuffle had been made, when the shrill song, or rather scream, of the fair bayaderes no longer sounded in our ears, and we were free to adjourn to our long-deferred dinner. An excellent repast had been provided and set out in the large hall, and soon all the visitors to the Valley were feasting under the marble canopy, where in former days the royal descendants of the proud line of Timour were wont to entertain their guests. The Maharajah himself did not personally act the host, his religion being a bar to any conviviality with the stranger; so the Resident took upon himself that office, and after the toast of 'The Queen, proposed the health of the prince, and thanked him in the name of all for the enjoyable entertainment he had offered. Shortly after we took our departure, and the stillness of the lake was broken by the noise of numerous paddles belonging to the boats that were bearing back the revellers to their respective homes. The night was fine and bright, and the moon, then at full, with her soft light lit up the whole landscape. And it was a charming scene—a lake of silver, set in a framing of dark and gloomy mountains; the calm, still waters unmoved or unruffled, and the silence of the night unbroken save by the dash of oars, whose dripping blades gave out showers of glittering drops, that flashed and sparkled in the soft, clear light reflected from the glorious orb on high. There was a race across the lake among the numerous boats, and at this sport we rather excelled; for, anticipating some such idea on the part of the English community, our boat's crew had been increased from six to eight men, and being a small, light craft, the exertions of the rowers, stimulated by promises of pecuniary reward, caused it to fly through the water. Distancing all competitors, we speedily arrived about the first at our temporary dwelling, which we had quitted that afternoon for what had resulted in an agreeable and amusing entertainment.

The Harri Parbat, an isolated hill between two and three hundred feet high, standing outside the city on its northern side, is well worth visiting; for a splendid view is to be obtained from its summit, which is occupied by the fort, also deserving inspection. Built by Akbar in 1590, it is surrounded by a stone wall of about three miles in length; and the fort itself, erected of the same material, consists of two wings placed nearly at right angles to each other, and a separate square building with a bastion at each end just below the western wing. It contains nothing very remarkable within its walls except a few old guns, and an ancient temple. All the buildings used as barracks for a small garrison are in a half-ruined condition, the whole place being very different to what it was in the days of the Moguls, when it served to overawe the capital of their lately-acquired possession.

There yet remains to be noticed in the environs of the city the great and small parade-grounds, the gun factory, and the Ram Bagh, which contains the tomb of Gulab Singh, father of the present ruler. The small parade-ground is situated on the opposite side of the river to the English quarter, and just above the first bridge, being easily reached in a short walk down an avenue of poplar trees, after landing at a small ghât close to the summer palace or pavilion. On this ground the reviews take place, and the game of 'choghan,' or polo, is played. To see that game as we saw it played by the men of a Balti regiment was exciting enough, and rather different to the milder imitation familiar to us in India and at home; for Baltistân, one of the countries included in the Jamoo and Kashmir territories, is the home of polo. It is the national game, all classes of society engaging in it as if it was one of the chief objects of their life. Their children at a very early age play it on foot, until old and strong enough to take their part in the *mêlée* on horseback. Polo is a very ancient game; for it was played in Turkey in the twelfth century, and in India during the reign of the Moguls; while, although we possess no reliable accounts of its history as regards Baltistân and Dârdistân, it is certain that for very many years the people of these countries have been passionately fond of it. There are certain points of difference between their game and the one played by Europeans, and there is no maximum or minimum number of players, which varies according to the size of the ground. In the game we saw, which was got up for the especial benefit of the visitors, the Maharajah himself being present, there were twenty-five picked men on each side. It was commenced by one with the ball in his hand starting off at full gallop, and when in the middle of the ground throwing it up in the air, and striking it as well as he could towards the goal of his opponents. His own side and his opponents followed close behind, and soon commenced the struggle for the second stroke, or the carrying the ball onward by successive strokes towards the desired direction, in which they are very expert. Their ponies too are well trained, following it in every turn, and to the best of their speed entering into the spirit of the game with apparently the same zest as their masters. It is very exciting to watch one very well-mounted man driving the ball before him, and closely pursued by friends and foes. Then, when it gets checked, a *mêlée* ensues, and crowding, pushing, and hooking of sticks, which is allowable, is the order of the day, until by some chance the ball gets clear, and is carried away by some expert hand, when another race begins to make or save the game. All this time the music has been playing wildly; for it is considered impossible to play well without its cheering influence, and the drums and the long horns that compose the band strike in with especial vigour on the taking off, and on each rush or *mêlée*. When the ball is caught, and the game won, the sounds of victory are given with great force, and so the play continues, until one side, having won the greater number out of the appointed total to be played, are hailed as victors, and the concluding part of the proceedings takes place.

This is a ceremony which is decidedly great fun, more particularly to the victors, the vanquished not appreciating it so fully. The winning side ride up and collect in front of the higher dignitaries present, the band playing what is understood to be a howl of triumph, a sort of Asiatic version of the 'Conquering Hero,' and then, dismounting, receive with undisguised looks of glee the salaams or homage of their late opponents. This seems to afford them immense satisfaction, which is increased by largesse from the princes and others present, and if particularly elated, as they would appear to have been in the game we witnessed, a grotesque dance follows, accompanied by hideous grimaces and pointed gestures to mark their joy; while the vanquished party slink off in silence to hide their diminished heads.

The larger parade-ground is nearer the city, not far from the gun-factory, neither of which need description; while the tomb of Gulab Singh, in the Ram Bagh, is on the direct road to Shupiyan, about a mile beyond the parade-ground, and can be easily visited, if it has not already been, on the march from Ramoo to Srinagar, when making for that capital by the old and imperial Pir Panjál route.

CHAPTER VIII.

Tour of the Valley—Objects of Interest in the North-western Portion of Kashmir—Departure from Srinagar—Our Course down the River—Sunnybawan—Shadipore—Hindu Fanatics—The Sind River—Ganderbal—The Sind Valley—The Lâdâkh Road—Zozila Pass—Wangat—Ruins at Wangat—The Haramuk Mountain—The Gungabal Lake—Sonamarg, or Golden Meadow—The Noroo Canal—The Manasbal Lake—The Lakes of Kashmir—Canal leading to Manasbal Lake—A Mosquito Incident—Fleas in Kashmir—Our Anguish—Beautiful Scene on the Lake—The Lake and its Surroundings—Scene at Sunset—A Hindu Fakir digging his own Grave—Our Remarks—His Delight—Sumbal—Continue our Way—Hajan—The Woolar Lake—Bandipoor—The Gales on the Lake—The Lanka—Hill of Shakuradin—Course of the Jhelam—Sopoor.

HAVING now well-nigh exhausted the sights of the capital and environs, we proceed further afield and commence the tour of the Valley, taking the north-western portion first, in order that we may make our way to Gulmarg, a justly favourite sanitarium for visitors during the months of July and August, when residence in the capital or moving about the country is not attended with the same comfort as during the other periods of the year in Kashmir. The principal objects of interest in this portion of the country are the Sind river, which is navigable as far as Ganderbal, whence the Sind Valley can be visited; the Manasbal and Woolar lakes; Gulmarg, Sonamarg, and the Lolab; perhaps one of the prettiest parts of the whole province. The commencement of this tour may be made by water, and engaging two 'doongahs' for self and servants, one can proceed comfortably enough, orders being given, if required, for the heavy baggage and horses, under the charge of a trusty guide, to be marched by land, with instructions when to meet the party in the boats. Dropping down the river from our encampment—our home for some time past—at an early hour of the morning, we proceed on our way through the city, and after traversing its whole length emerge into the open country, which presents a lovely appearance. The rising sun lights up with its glowing rays the bare and rugged sides of the surrounding mountains, and throws a halo of light on their lofty peaks. Fields of rich crops slope down to the banks of the river on either side, with range beyond range of mountains for background, those in the distance and the loftiest covered with glistening snow; the sides of others clothed with masses of trees and luxuriant vegetation, a marked contrast to their neighbours, standing out bare and rugged, yet sharply defined in the clear morning air, with nothing to hide their desolate but majestic beauty. Floating leisurely down the stream, we pass the pretty grove of Sunnybawan, with its group of poplar and chenar trees growing close to the water's edge; and in about four hours from the time of leaving Srinagar approach closer to the mountains, which at first had seemed so distant, enabling us to obtain a very good view of the wild and extensive range whose precipitous sides form the boundaries of the Sind Valley. The entrance of this valley is plainly discernible, giving us a fair idea of the scenery of a gorge thus formed, which apart from its picturesque beauty is interesting as containing the Lâdâkh road, the great commercial highway between India, Kashmir, and the towns of Central Asia. A little further on and we arrive abreast of the small village of Shadipore, a name which signifies 'the place of marriage,' and here denotes the junction of the cold and icy waters of the Sind river with the Jhelam. These points of junction of different rivers have from time immemorial been held sacred by the Hindus, who generally erect a place of worship near by. And such is not wanting here; for the ruins of an old temple stand on a solid mass of masonry in the bed of the Jhelam, immediately below the meeting of the waters. This ancient fane, dedicated to Mahadeo, although deserted and peaceful-looking enough to-day, has in its time witnessed some awful scenes; for countless acts of self-immolation have been committed on this spot — the misguided devotees plunging from its base into the river, thinking to gain by this act of suicide eternal bliss in the future state, conferred on them by the supernatural agency of the sacred waters, beneath whose waves they find a willing death.

The Sind as it joins the Jhelam is nearly 100 yards wide, and deep enough in the early part of the season to allow a boat to proceed all the way to Ganderbal, a journey of some hours from its mouth. If the time of the year is not favourable to its navigation, Ganderbal can be reached easily from Srinagar, whence it is distant about fourteen miles, the road winding along the northern side of the city, and through Naoshera, famous for its paper manufactories, passing on the way several old ruins, and at one place large masses of shingle on the hillside, testifying to the truth of the ancient lake theory of the country. Ganderbal is a small village sheltered beneath a spur of the mountains, where it is usual to make a halt to complete preparations for a

To face page 181

From a photograph by Mr. H. Simpson. Stanford's Geogl. Estabt.

THE SIND VALLEY VIEW BETWEEN SONAMARG AND BALTAL

journey through the whole or a part of the Sind Valley. This long and very narrow valley, leading up to the centre of the great snowy range of mountains that separates Kashmir from Lâdâkh, takes its name from the Sind river, which rises in the mountains some twenty miles or so from the head of the valley, into which it enters through a deep defile to the eastward, and is a swiftly-rushing and icy-cold stream. The scenery throughout the valley is very beautiful, in fact by many it is held to be the most beautiful of all the minor valleys that debouch upon the main valley of Kashmir, while its climate, cool and pleasant, renders it an enjoyable place to wander about in during the unpleasant months, the sojourn of the sportsman being enhanced by the certainty of finding something in the way of big game to repay his trouble. It is said, although I myself did not test this personally, that some of the finest sport is to be met with in this direction, and on the higher ranges of the mountains that surround it. The widest part of the valley is at its commencement, and here for several miles the scenery is perhaps at its best. On either side are loftv mountains, many with summits tipped with snow, the lower portion of those on the left bank of the river covered with dense forests of fir, spruce, and deodar, extending for several thousand feet up their sides, while along the lower edge a brighter belt of green is formed by trees that grow under more sheltered and favourable circumstances. On the other bank, the north side of the valley, the aspect varies, for the southern outlook is not favourable to vegetation, and the sides of the mountains are but grassy slopes, and higher up are rocks, precipitous cliffs, and ravines. Many smaller valleys open into the main valley, both on this and the opposite side, while at the very base of the hills on either bank of the river a natural plantation is formed of walnut, peach, mulberry, and other fruit trees.

Dotted along by the river are small villages or isolated cottages, surrounded by small patches of ground under cultivation, and each with its orchard of fine and profusely-laden fruit trees. Along the right bank passes the Lâdâkh road, Leh, the capital of that province, being distant some 240 miles from Gahderbal—twenty long marches, in one of which the Zozila pass has to be crossed. The journey altogether is rather fatiguing, although taken by many of the visitors as a part of their tour in the Happy Valley. We did not perform the feat, much as I should have liked to have visited Leh, and seen the Lâdâkhis in their own home, so different from the country we have been visiting. Then we should have found ourselves completely in Tibet; for this ancient kingdom was one of the many annexed to form the territory of the Maharajah of Jamoo and Kashmir, having been before that event tributary to that far-famed but rarely seen personage, the Grand Lama of Tibet, at Llâsa.

If one does not proceed the whole way to Leh, Sonamarg, at the head of the valley, is usually the termination of the trip, and a very enjoyable week or ten days may be passed in marching to this spot by easy stages, halting when suitable ground is to be found for the nightly encampment, and paying a short visit to the ruins above Wangat, in a minor valley opening into the larger one, and distant about ten miles from Ganderbal. This offshoot of the Sind Valley is a few miles long only, and very narrow, confined and hemmed in by very high and rugged mountains. At its upper extremity is the small village of Wangat, and some two miles beyond is Rajdainbul, the ruin of a very fine stone temple, enclosed by a wall, and of great antiquity, resembling that of Martand in architecture. (The latter will be found described in the record of our visit to the other portion of the country.) About 150 yards further is another similar structure, and close by is a holy spring much frequented by pilgrims, who visit it on their road to the sacred lake of Gungabal, situated upon the top of the Haramuk mountain, whose lofty peak, nearly 17,000 feet in height, overlooks and overshadows the valley. The ascent to the lake is a stiff pull, and the piece of water itself, which is one of the mountain sources of the Jhelam, is something over a mile long and less than a quarter wide, lying under the wildest and most lofty eminence of the mountain.

Returning, after visiting the ruins, from Wangat to Ganderbal, it is best to proceed leisurely through the valley to Sonamarg, a distance of some forty miles, the road passing by the side of the river, and near to three or four small villages, where, however, supplies of any sort are difficult to procure. Beyond a place called Gagangîr, about ten miles from Sonamarg, the valley becomes narrower, a perfect gorge in fact, through which the waters dash and tumble on their troubled course; and the path we are following is carried among the large boulders that lie between its right bank and the overhanging cliff which hems it in. Some miles beyond the gorge is left, and more open ground reached; and the river being crossed, a steep path of a few hundred feet or so conducts to the mountain down of Sonamarg, the 'golden meadow,' or 'pleasant plain as it is sometimes called. And a very pleasant spot to linger on it is—a tract of beautiful undulating down, with numerous dells, surrounded by hillocks or grassy mounds. These charming nooks are covered with long, thick grass, and numerous wild flowers grow plentifully all about; and the slopes of the hillocks are clothed with silver fir, sycamore, birch, and other trees, beautifully intermingled, while rugged rocks here and there project through the green covering of the grassy mounds. The climate is delicious, and many remain encamped on this spot for some considerable time; for life on the 'marg' is very enjoyable.

However, deferring further description until our arrival at Gulmarg, we proceed to retrace our steps, and taking boat at Ganderbal, float down to Shadipore, the point on the Jhelam which we left to visit the Sind Valley and the ruined temples above Wangat. Immediately below Shadipore the Noroo canal leaves the left bank of the river, and dividing into two branches, conducts, the one towards Pattan, the other to the Woolar lake, and forms, when the water is high enough, the shortest route between the capital and Báramúla. Two or three old and ruined pleasure-gardens are passed on the right bank; but there is nothing of more interest until we arrive at Sumbal, a small village, at which there is a fine bridge across the river, here of some considerable width. A quarter of a mile further on a small canal opens on the right bank, close to another small village, completely sheltered and surrounded by fine mulberry trees. Following this channel for a mile, we emerge into the open water of the place we have come to visit, the far-famed and beautiful Manasbal lake.

Numerous lakes are found about Kashmir, both in the Valley itself or on the surrounding mountains. Of the former, the Dal, or city lake, which we have already visited, is perhaps the principal and most interesting, on account of its historical associations; while the Woolar is by far the largest. The Manasbal, however, although the smallest, is undoubtedly the most charming of all, both in itself and in the beauty of the scenery around; its calm, pellucid depths lying embosomed amidst these lofty mountains, which aid so materially the formation of those scenes of loveliness that have gained for this country its just and enviable renown.

Of the mountain lakes, many of which are curious as being found at such a height, the Konsa Nág, on the top of the Punjál, and the Sheesha Nág, situated on the path to the Ambernath cave, are the principal, and will be referred to further on. The Gangabal, another of some size, has been already visited from the ruins above Wangat, and there are several others, such as the Mar Sar, Tar Sar, Sona Sar, Hokar Sar, Nila Nag, and the Deo Sar, small sheets of water on different parts of the rocky barrier that surrounds Kashmir, but which call for no further remark, as they are not of interest enough to attract a special visit to their shores.

The canal leading from the river to the Manasbal lake is only about a mile long; but being shallow, and its surface covered with aquatic plants and weeds, slow progress is made, and one usually attended by the unpleasant consequences which follow the disturbance of the leaves that form the verdant covering of so many of the watery channels of the country. One is positively almost eaten up by mosquitoes, which, with fleas, sand-flies, and a few other interesting insects, are the very curse of the land, and the one crumpled rose-leaf in the otherwise even enjoyment of a tour in the Happy Valley. Of fleas the visitor sees, or rather feels, as many in a week as he is ever likely to do for the rest of his natural life; for enter a house, or pitch your tent, no matter where, they seem to rise by magic out of the ground, and until you really become in a measure used to the infliction a night's sound sleep in Kashmir is a thing only of the past; so numerous are they, and so eager to feast upon you, that the oft-quoted remark made by an author and traveller in these parts, is only too applicable to the situation. So many and so ravenous were the fleas that nightly assailed his couch, that, if they had been only unanimous in their actions, they were, said he, in sufficient force to have pulled him out of bed!

Mosquitoes are equally numerous, more particularly on the margins of the lakes and rivers, and in the narrow water-courses, where, sheltered by the leaves of the lilies and other plants, they pass their uneventful lives, rousing, however, into extreme activity when anything in the shape of prey comes within reach. This was fully and painfully exemplified in our case when we forced our way through the mass of vegetation that obstructed our passage to the Manasbal lake. Of these plagues of the East we had of course some experience in India, for there are few visitors to that country that have not endured at certain seasons of the year the stinging bite, followed by the unsightly swelling, of these insect pests. But our former knowledge of their habits and customs was now about to be largely increased; for deeming probably that only a little knowledge was dangerous, they apparently considered it their bounden duty to impart the fullest entomological and experimental demonstration as to their power of suction, and their capability of absorbing the vital fluid of their victims. They descended on us in clouds, and we were soon enveloped in a perfect mist of mosquitoes, all hastening to the unwonted feast that lay so temptingly spread before them, decidedly more to their taste than the juice of some tough leaf of the water-lily. If 'seeing is believing,' that truism must hold good in this instance; for without actual proof it would have been difficult to imagine the situation. We were, particularly on the barer and more exposed portions of the face and limbs, literally covered with these fierce and ravenous creatures, whose thin and supple bodies actually quivered with delight, as, swooping down with their clear, trumpet-like blast, already heralding victory, they fixed on the skin, and soon were rapt in the enjoyment of an epicurean feast, preferring death rather than removal; for they allowed themselves to be touched or handled whilst thus engaged without showing any desire or inclination for flight. The agonies endured by our lightly-clothed servants and the semi-nude natives that propelled the boat must have been acute; for to us, protected as we were, the sensation experienced was that of being subjected to a shower bath of red hot needles. They even penetrated our clothes, which offered but feeble resistance to their sharp lances; and to increase the torture of the moment was the reflection of what would follow in the form of an irritated skin, caused by the poisonous bites, while, in the case of my companion, thoughts as to the effect on her personal appearance the following day must likewise be added. Self-preservation is a great law of nature, and not sharing the ideas of the followers of Jaina, to whom even insect life is sacred, we attempted to protect ourselves against the ravages of our foes by lighting a fire of green wood, the smoke of which is considered efficacious in arresting their approach, causing them to fall stupified into the flames. But unfortunately the remedy was as bad as the disease; and a short trial of squatting amidst the volumes of acrid smoke produced by the experiment, like two hams undergoing the process of curing, was sufficient to prove that we must endure the mosquito plague with fortitude, or be choked in the reek of our own raising. Fortunately the open water of the lake was not far distant, and encountering a slight breeze on clearing the canal, our enemies were wafted slowly and reluctantly away. Our delight at this, probably owing to a natural spirit of vindictiveness, was largely increased by the knowledge that, owing to their greed, their wings could hardly sustain the weight of their now swollen bodies, and that retribution in the form of a watery grave must undoubtedly overtake many of their number.

On emerging upon the open water of the Manasbal, we were, however, rewarded for the ordeal through which we had passed, which was quickly forgotten in the ecstasy of delight created by the aspect of the spot and its surroundings, which burst upon our view immediately we entered upon its calm, deep surface. The scene was one of such great and exceeding loveliness that words are but poor means for conveying any real idea of the glories of this apparently enchanted region, as it appeared that evening. It was the hour of sunset; the sky showed bright and clear, save where a few fleecy clouds were drifting slowly towards the west, tinged with the reddish orange-colour reflected by the rays of the now rapidly disappearing orb of day, which, although half-hidden by the lofty mountains of the western range, still afforded in its expiring glory sufficient dazzling light to throw the most exquisite tints and shades upon and around the surrounding scenery. The lake upon which we were floating lay spread out before us—an oval silvery sheet of crystal, reflecting on its untroubled surface a perfect picture of the works of nature by which it was encircled. On our left was an elevated table-land, and crouching under its shadow was the small and pretty village of Manasbal; while above and beyond, on higher ground, stood another evidence of man's presence in the ruins of the Badshah Bagh, an old palace and garden built by the Mogul Emperor Jehangir, for the use of his wife, the fair and celebrated 'Light of the Harem.' On the right was a low range of hills, extending from the lofty mountains on the north-east, with a conical peak, the Aha-Thang, towering aloft to an altitude of nearly 7,000 feet, an object plainly discernible from many other parts of the Valley. In front we gazed from the calm still waters of the lake upon a rugged range of rocky heights, whose precipitous sides were clothed with large forests of pine and other trees, while their peaks, bare and defiant, lifted their heads towards the azure sky, affording a marked contrast to the lesser ridge below. This, lined with walnut, chestnut, sycamore, and various other species, gave passage through a picturesque valley to a small stream that, in the form of a foaming cataract, finally dashed wildly over a steep limestone cliff into the lake below, which lay otherwise in placid beauty, surrounded and guarded by the rocky sentinels that have kept watch and ward over its depths unchanged and unchanging through countless ages.

On turning to catch a last view of the setting sun, we beheld in the distance the great Pir Panjál, with its spotless mantle of everlasting snow now appearing of a brilliant rose-colour, adding splendour and solemnity to a scene of such unspeakable beauty, that it was with a feeling of awe and reverence we gazed upon this glimpse of an almost earthly paradise. Alas, all too soon for us, gradually and slowly it underwent a transformation. Imperceptibly the colours deepened, then subsided. Twilight approached, and a change from azure and pink to a deep grey tint rapidly appeared, while, slowly rising in majestic dignity, shedding over all a soft and gentle radiance, appeared the moon, like a disc of silver, hastening to take the place in the firmament which her more fiery rival had so lately vacated. Slowly and reluctantly we bade farewell to this lovely spectacle, one of the happiest memories of our tour, and continued our course towards the further end of the lake, which, elliptical in shape, is about three miles long by one mile wide. The water is clear and soft, of a deep green colour, and in many places upwards of forty feet in depth, although, according to a Hindu legend, it is reckoned unfathomable, it being related that many years ago a holy man spent the best part of his life in constructing a line of sufficient length to reach the bottom, but not succeeding in his attempt threw himself in despair into the depths, never to rise again, an act of self-sacrifice considered most meritorious by his countrymen, who continue to hold his memory in the highest veneration.

The lake is even at the present day not without its attraction to the pious followers of Brahma; for on its margin a Hindu fakir, a very holy man, has for many years resided, employing his leisure in the interesting and laudable occupation of digging his own grave. Evidently of an ambitious nature, or considering that his pious and sanctified life entitle his remains to a more fitting mausoleum than they would otherwise obtain, he has, with infinite care and trouble, constructed a large cave out of the solid rock, on the face of the mountain behind his present dwelling-place. The worthy recluse himself showed us over his future resting-place, imparting the fact that he thought it was now about sufficiently complete for its intended purpose. In this we heartily concurred; for it opened with a tunnel fifty feet long from the entrance, and in size sufficient to allow of two grown people to walk side by side upright. This passage led into a species of vaulted chamber, in the centre of which was the space already excavated to receive the corpse of our smiling guide. He appeared very proud and happy when we admired his handiwork, and observed that it was undoubtedly, as far as dryness and warmth were concerned, the best place of interment in the whole of the country! Regarding his future state he appeared to entertain no doubts; for he further informed us that, having now completed his task, he waited impatiently for the time when it should be applied to its destined use, and himself commence the life of bliss assured through a long period of penance and austerity upon earth. Already a saint, his death in the odour of sanctity would cause his memory to be held in veneration by his countrymen for long years to come, and make the place of his interment a holy sepulchre, to which they would repair in large numbers and worship at his shrine.

The excellent old man looked, however, as if he

had yet some years of life before him; for he was hale and hearty, and although wrapped in perpetual thoughts of future happiness, was not unmindful or above more earthly matters. He demanded baksheesh in return for the show like an ordinary mortal, and invoked for our liberality numerous blessings on our heads as being cherishers and protectors of the poor, supplementing his prayers by an offering of some very fine grapes and peaches, in the cultivation of which he has long been famous. Their sale, with the addition of the gifts of the pious and curious, afford him, I should imagine, a very comfortable maintenance.

There are some very good spots on the margin of the lake, at its upper end, suitable for encamping purposes, and many linger here for some days. But apart from its scenery there is nothing of special interest, so we proceed with our tour on the following day, gaining the river Jhelam at the point at which we had left it, and by the same canal, the scene of our misery. We feared a repetition, but happily escaped, a fact attributable perhaps to our former foes being engaged in sleeping off the effects of their unwonted debauch. After leaving Sumbal, we continue our course down the Jhelam, meeting nothing remarkable to attract our attention until we arrive about half-way between the village we have just left and the Woolar lake, our intended destination, where, on the left bank of the river, stands the village of Hajan. This place is interesting as having been the probable site of Parihas-pur, a city founded by Lâlitâditya, about the year 714, of which, however, only a few ruins remain. Another three hours' journey and we enter upon the Woolar lake, the largest in the country, which is crossed by travellers on their way to Srinagar by the Marri route, as mentioned when speaking of that journey. It is truly a magnificent piece of water, about twelve miles long by eight broad, but is not of great depth, as only over a part of it does it exceed twelve feet, and in some places it is even shallower; and its surface here is covered with the lotus, singhara, and other water-plants. Its shores are verdant, but comparatively bare of trees, and they slope gradually down from the lofty range of mountains which surrounds it on the north-east, with numerous villages dotted about, the largest of which is Bandipoor, the starting-point of the route to Gilgit and Iskardo.

This village, or rather town, is of considerable size, situated on the north-eastern side of the lake, a little over a mile from its margin, and to it we will direct our boat, provided always that the weather is fine, for, like all lakes surrounded by mountains, the Woolar is liable to the influence of sudden and furious gales, converting its usually calm surface into an angry and raging storm-tossed sea, upon which the usual boats of the country find it difficult to live.

Before reaching this village, in fact almost as soon as we enter upon the lake, we come to the only island it contains, the Lanka, raised and shaped by the Mohammedan king Zinalabudin, who, it is affirmed, constructed it out of the ruins of a city, said to have existed where water only now is. Whether there is any truth in this legend it would be hard to say, but undoubtedly the substratum of the island consists of such an enormous mass of blocks of stone that if brought from a distance considerable trouble and ingenuity must have been observed in the task, and much time taken to construct that which was comparatively easy enough to do when the materials lay ready to hand. The surface of this artificial island, which is quadrangular in shape, occupies about four acres, the ground being covered with trees, and plentifully bestrewn with fragments of sculptured stones and broken pillars, remains of buildings, walls, and ghâts that at one time adorned this curious isle. At its eastern extremity stands yet a considerable portion of what was originally a Hindu palace, interesting as being similar in architecture to the ruins at Martand, which were certainly erected long before the time of the monarch who originated this island. He has left, however, an evidence of his religion in the form of an old Mohammedan cemetery, inside which is a stone slab with a Persian inscription, stating that the Lanka was constructed by himself about the year 1411 of our era. The island from a little distance looks exceedingly picturesque, the surrounding mountains forming an excellent background.

Chief among the eminences that encircle the lake stands the hill of Shukarudin, at the edge of the spur on its western side, some little distance away. Towards this, passing by the town of Bandipoor, where there is nothing to detain us, we make our way, and sailing past Aloos, halt at Kewnus, a village some three miles off, whence the ascent to its summit can be easily effected. If time allows, this should most certainly be done; for a magnificent view of the whole of the lake and surrounding country is the reward for the rather steep and rough but short journey to the top of the hill. The 'zearat' or shrine of the Babu Shukarudin stands on the summit, some three hundred feet above the water, and from it the Woolar is seen in all its beauty and grandeur. Looking eastwards the Lanka stands out boldly and clearly defined on the calm surface of the lake; and carrying the eye still further beyond it the glittering waters of Manasbal are plainly perceptible, lying under the shadow of the Aha-Thang; while towards the south the towns of Sopoor and Báramúla are seen; and beyond again the high range of hills which overlooks the downs of Gulmarg, that charming spot towards which we are hastening as fast as the interesting objects on our way allow. The river Jhelam too, which pursues its course in traversing the whole length of the Valley through the Woolar, is to be seen entering the lake at its eastern side, and, merging into its waters for some considerable distance, can be again traced, where after its passage it issues again as a fine open stream, two hundred yards in width, a little above the town of Sopoor, winding to the westward flows past Báramúla, and shortly after leaves the Valley for the plains of India.

Sopoor is an ancient and dilapidated town, built

upon both sides of the Jhelam where it leaves the lake, and although a good place for fishing, contains nothing remarkable to detain us. Therefore, instead of proceeding any further down the river, which in a few hours' row would bring us to the town of Báramúla, we now strike across country and make for Lalpoor, distant some sixteen miles, and the largest and principal village in that pretty part of the Vale of Kashmir called the Lolab.

CHAPTER IX.

The Road to Lalpoor—The Lolab—Kashmir Villages—The Kangri—Mulberry Trees—Silk Cultivation in the Valley—Silk-producing Insects—Bears in Kashmir—Their Carnivorous Propensities—Varieties of Game in the Valley—Sport in Kashmir—The Tiger Cat—The Wild Dog—The Barasing—The Musk-deer—The Markor—The Khakur—The Surrow—The Ibex—Their Habitats—Wild Fowl in the Valley—Singing Birds—Birds of Prey—Eagles—Hawks—Monkeys—Hares—No Monkeys or Hares found in the Valley—Probable Reason of their Absence—The Alpine Hare.

THE road from Sopoor to Lalpoor is for the first nine miles smooth and level, and full of picturesque beauty, but becomes rather steep and rough when that distance has been traversed, as after leaving Arwan, a small village at the foot of the hills, a range of about 8,000 feet high has to be crossed in order to reach our destination, distant about four miles from its foot. Arrived at Lalpoor, we find ourselves in the heart of the Lolab, as pretty a part as any in the whole of Kashmir, situated in the north-eastern side of the province, in that division of it called Kamraj It consists of an undulating green and fertile valley some twelve miles long, with a varying width of from two or three hundred yards to nearly three miles, completely encircled by hills, covered for the most part with forests of pine, deodar, and other trees. Its altitude being some 600 feet, it possesses a cool and invigorating climate, and for general fertility is unsurpassed in the Valley. A gurgling stream traverses its entire length, and numerous villages and farm-houses are found dotted about in every part, it being a favourite spot for farmers, although, owing perhaps to the grinding system of taxation which prevails, there is not so much land under cultivation as there should be.

The villages in this locality are good examples of Kashmir villages in general, which, although untidy in detail, are certainly picturesque, the cottages standing detached, and not crowded together as seen in India, and all with groves of fruit trees, which surround and shelter the dwellings. The houses are usually two-storied, with walls of wood or mud, and a low sloping gabled roof of thatch or shingle, and generally possess a balcony on the upper part, which, sheltered by the overhanging eaves, makes an extra room, enabling the tenant to utilize, as is frequently found to be the case, the lower portion of his domicile as a stable for his cattle. One peculiarity that cannot fail to be noticed in all houses in Kashmir, is the total absence of chimneys; for although a few possess fire-places, the smoke is allowed to escape through a hole in the wall or roof, and not by the usual channel that obtains in all civilized countries. Fires are, however, but rarely used by the Kashmiris except for cooking purposes; for they have a plan that may be termed an institution of the country, which renders them independent even of household fires for a protection against cold. This is the universal 'kângrî,' an earthern pot set in a basket, and filled with live charcoal, which all classes carry, holding it beneath their loose garments against any portion of their bodies that requires warmth. A primitive arrangement truly, but one that apparently answers the purpose; for with it they brave the cold of winter attired in the costume worn during the warmer months when out of doors; and when in the house a number of these burners, round which they sit, afford them as much warmth as a wood fire, their only fuel, coals being totally unknown in the Valley.

The mulberry tree is very common in the Lolab, and generally all over the country; and with such an abundant supply of the first necessity in the cultivation of silk, and with such a favourable climate, it is a little remarkable that this great branch of industry is not prosecuted with greater vigour than at present. A certain quantity of silk is yearly produced in Kashmir, from worms preserved and fed in this division of the Valley, and elsewhere, but nothing like what could be done, considering the first means for its production are so ready to hand—quantities of the natural food of the silkworm, in a locality so favourably situated as to climate that the foliage is in readiness for feeding the young worms when they are first hatched from the eggs. I cannot with any certainty state what variety of the silkworm is found in this country, as it was late in the season when I visited an establishment for their cultivation, and the worm had passed into its pupa state; but from the description I should imagine it was the common kind, the caterpillar of the *Bombyx mori*, the silkworm moth, a native of India, but plentiful in other parts of the world, notably in China and elsewhere. There are numerous species belonging to this genus, and other genera of the family *Bombycidæ*, to be found in India and adjacent parts, whose chrysalides, enclosed in a cocoon of silk, give to most of the species such a great economical importance. But of the silk-producing insects as used in manufacture, only about five out of the eighteen varieties existing in the country, generally on certain parts of the Himalaya mountains, are of any importance; and of that number only two, the common silkworm, and the true *Tusseh Antherœa Paphia*, or 'Tussur moth,' produce silk that can be easily wound off the cocoon, and whose cultivation is attended with any great advantage or profit.

It is stated that in China the silkworm is sometimes reared upon trees in the open air, showing very little desire to wander from the place of its birth; but it is usual in that as in all other countries to raise them in buildings constructed for the purpose. Such a building we visited in Kashmir, and found it a large, long, wooden, barn-like erection, carefully covered in so as to exclude moisture, with its interior divided into compartments, or tier upon tier of shelves, such as one sees in the garrets of English farm-houses for storing apples and other fruits. On these shelves the eggs are hatched by the natural heat of the climate, and the silkworms are fed with the leaves of the mulberry until they attain their full development, and then spin in the corners of the shelves, or on little contrivances placed above them for that purpose. These trays or shelves are quite open, as it is not necessary to enclose them in any wav: for it is an interesting peculiarity of this valuable species of moth, that neither in its caterpillar state, as long as food is fresh and abundant, nor in the winged state, does it show that restless disposition or desire to wander away which is so common to so many others. After spinning the cocoons are collected, and those few selected for the production of the perfect insect, necessary for the maintenance and increase of the stock, carefully set aside. The others are plunged into hot water or baked, in order to kill the enclosed chrysalis, to prevent perforation and spoiling of the silk from the moth forcing its way out. The silk is then wound off and disposed of, and the building, swept and garnished, is shut up to await the hatching of the crop of eggs, simultaneously with the appearance of the leaves of the mulberry-trees that surround its site, the following year.

The mulberry and other fruit-trees in the Lolab possess also great attractions in the proper season to another species of living creature, not quite so innocent nor so simple in its habits as the one lately described; for it is famous for the number of bears that visit the trees to feast upon the luscious product of their branches. Their greed oftentimes proves their destruction; for, engaged in the pleasant occupation of taking their dessert, they fall easy victims to any one who likes to take the trouble of shooting them as they sit perched up aloft, or watching for them on their way to and from the scene of their enjoyment. Bears are found in all parts of Kashmir, and although not so numerous as formerly —every European visiting the Valley being desirous and usually fulfilling his desire of taking a shot at them—are still very common, more particularly in the part of the country just described, in the Nowboog valley, and on the slopes of the Pir Panjál. There are two varieties of this animal met with in this country. The brown or red variety, which generally resides high up in the mountains, and the black, lower down, also to be found during the summer and autumn near the villages or patches of cultivated ground searching for fruit and vegetables. Although grass, roots, and fruit form their chief diet, and they are usually classed as herbivorous animals, there is no doubt that they are partly carnivorous, as the shepherd in this country knows to his cost; for many sheep are killed and eaten by them, and any sick or wounded animal, such as a cow or horse, that falls within their reach is readily killed by master Bruin, and a hearty meal made off the carcase. Bears in Kashmir, and I suppose in all other countries where they are to be found, seem to possess the power of smell to a remarkable degree, and it behoves the hunter to be very careful to avoid their exercising this faculty, or success will not attend his efforts to secure a skin. It is said, but I cannot answer for the truth of the assertion, that they have an inordinate craving for the flesh of the unclean animal, and that any traveller in this region will most probably have his tent or hut invaded by a bear, if he himself or his servants leaves an open tin of bacon, such as the Englishman loves in the East, lying about. That they certainly come very near, if not into, the abode of man in this country I can well affirm; for at one place our servants, who usually slept outside our tent, displayed great unwillingness to do so, on account, as they said, of the bears, and crowded instead, in a compact body for mutual protection, into a small one used for the storage of our luggage and supplies. And again, when encamped in a pine forest on a slope of the Panjál, we were roused from sleep by our little dog barking most furiously, and endeavouring to get at something under our camp-bed, which finally in the confusion escaped under the fly of the tent, and which, although I cannot affirm it as a fact, it being dark at the time, was thought both by myself and my servants, who pursued it for some little distance, to be no less than a small bear.

This animal, although it affords some slight sport and more amusement to the sportsman, is but one of the many varieties of game to be met with in Kashmir and adjoining countries, and which, although not so plentiful as in former days, yet affords to those who fear neither hard work nor exposure as good sport as the heart of man can desire. Of late years so much shooting has been carried on in the more accessible parts of the Valley, that to insure good bags being made it is incumbent on the hunter to go now further afield, and seek in the regions more inaccessible to the ordinary traveller for the trophies of the chase, which are nowhere more marked and varied than in the country now under consideration. Regarding the best time for shooting in and about Kashmir, from the middle of April to the beginning of July, and from September to the end of November, are perhaps the chief months of the year, heavy rain intervening between the two periods; while the best ground is also at that time covered with flocks and herds sent up from the lower parts of the Valley for grazing purposes, with the result of disturbing and driving away all the game in their vicinity.

Of the animals affording sport, leopards are found all round the Valley, and chiefly on the 'margs,' or mountain downs, where they occasionally commit great havoc amongst the sheep and cattle feeding on the rich pasture of these charming places. There is a species of wild or tiger-cat met with in the mountains, more particularly, I believe, about Poshiana and its vicinity, which is most beautifully marked, somewhat similar to the royal animal from which it derives its name. In size it is rather larger than the familiar tabby, and is of the most fierce and intractable disposition. A friend of ours had procured a live one in the mountains and brought it to Srinagar, where, secured by a chain to a collar round its neck, it was tied up near the door of his house; and being a young animal we entertained hopes of eventually taming it, and rendering it somewhat domesticated. But, despite all our efforts, its naturally fierce nature was not to be overcome by kindness or sweet persuasion, and it remained, as always, the most vindictive, cruel-looking specimen of the cat tribe I ever saw. I did not envy its possessor the task which lay before him, in carrying out his intention of taking the interesting creature to India, and subsequently to England. Tigers do not penetrate so far as the Valley, and the hyæna, so common in India, is rarely if ever met with here. This is also the case with the wolf, but jackals and foxes are abundant all over the Valley; a black variety of the latter has also been found in particular places.

The wild dogs, or 'dholes,' inhabitants of the deepest recesses of wild mountain forests, occasionally visit some parts of the Valley in large packs, more particularly the Wardwan; but as a rule they must be sought for further north, in Drás and Lâdâkh. This curious animal, of which there is no reason to think that any of them are the wild offspring of once domestic races, is in size between a wolf and a jackal, with long legs, sharp muzzle, pointed ears, and straight tail, usually of a light bay colour, and endowed with great courage, strength, and activity. They appear to be not incapable of domestication; but it is difficult to tame them. They are in habit gregarious, and hunt in packs, running down any animal they come across, and it is said, when pressed by hunger, have even destroyed children, and sometimes grown persons. One remarkable characteristic they possess, which may be said to be exhibited by the domesticated dog in a lesser degree, is their hostility to the feline race of animals, whom they destroy whenever the chance of so doing presents itself, as if they were the instruments appointed by Nature to keep within limit the superabundant increase of the great felinæ.

Of the deer tribe, the lordly 'bárasing, or 'hungul,' is found at certain seasons, more particularly towards the end of September, in many parts of Kashmir. This is the best time for shooting them, their horns being then fully developed. This fine stag is the nearest approach met with in the East to the red deer of Europe, and although larger and with bigger horns, in general appearance it resembles that variety somewhat closely. It is to be found and stalked in the elevated downs and forests of the country, and in the winter approaches close to the villages. At that time they are to be killed very easily; for they are weak from want of food, and cannot move quickly over the deep snow, and so fall an easy prey to the Kashmiri villagers, a mode of slaying them despised by the genuine sportsman. The musk-deer is found in all parts of Kashmir at a certain elevation, particularly along the Sind Valley, and is pretty generally distributed all over the elevated mountainous regions and table-lands of Central Asia. This type of the family *Moschidæ* differs, notwithstanding its name, from the *Cervidæ*, or deer, in its want of horns, and in the long canines of the males projecting beyond the lips, and used in the digging up of roots, and for fighting or defensive purposes. In this country, as elsewhere, it is much pursued, on account of its odoriferous secretion, known as musk, of which some quantity is yearly exported from Kashmir; but not so much as one would imagine, considering the number of the animals. Their habits, however, nocturnal and solitary, joined to their extreme timidity, render their destruction no easy matter. The 'khakar,' or barking deer, is found on the southern and western slopes of the Pir Panjál, and on this range the 'markhor' and 'surrow,' or mountain goat, are also met with, and the ibex affords good sport to such adventurous spirits as choose to follow this animal in its mountain retreats.

Such are the chief varieties of big game to be found in the Valley, and adjacent hills, and we now come to the winged kind, of which there are many species. In a country possessing so many rivers and lakes, it follows naturally that waterfowl in great abundance are to be met with in the winter months, when, to avoid the intense cold of the more northern regions of Central Asia, they seek this sheltered spot, departing, however, at the first sign of spring. Every species nearly of this description of game is well represented, particularly on the Woolar, and other lakes. Geese, ducks, teal, coots, moor-hens are all found, the two latter, and even certain varieties of ducks, remaining after the others have departed, to breed on the sedgy margins of the water. That magnificent bird, the royal partridge, three or four times the size of our common English variety, is found occasionally inhabiting the snowy Panjáls on both sides of the valley, and the black, grey, snow, and the 'chikore' or Himalayan red-legged variety, are met with, especially the latter, abundantly in many parts. Of pheasants, the varieties are the argus, 'moonhal,' 'koklas,' and the snow, all of which must be searched for in their favourite haunts, as also the quail, snipe, and plover. Several smaller birds are pretty common, such as the hoopoe, the mina, the cuckoo, and other varieties; but of singing-birds no great show is made. Excepting the Himalayan blackbird, and the bulbul, and a few others, with notes by no means full and musical, the forests and glades of Kashmir resound with little of the cheerful noise of the feathered songsters that add such a charm to similar places in England and elsewhere.

Birds of prey, as in other parts of the East, are common enough, and there are two or three varieties of the eagle to be met with, as well as many species of hawks, while crows similar in appearance to our own at home are abundant in every quarter of the province.

One curious fact in connection with this subject may be noticed in conclusion, and that is the total absence in any part of the Valley proper of monkeys or hares.

The first-named animal is common enough a few marches away from the country, but, as far as my recollection serves, was seen by us for the first time after crossing the Pir Panjál Pass on our return journey, the height of which or the cold experienced at certain times of the year, perhaps influences their habits in avoiding the Valley, which with its fruit trees and vines would prove a perfect paradise to this mischievous order. The reason why hares, common in India, and met with up to a few marches from Báramúla, avoid the Valley, is one of the most singular features connected with its natural history and difficult of explanation. Likelier ground for their harbouring and preservation could scarcely be found in any other part of the world, and our English hares would thrive and multiply there, I am certain, to an alarming extent. The Indian variety, however, I presume, in the same manner as the monkey, dreads the cold, and the little species met with in Tibet, on the other side, being a true Alpine hare, prefers to dwell among rocks, sand, and thorns, rather than seek the green and succulent food so dear to this class of animal generally, and which grows in wild and luxuriant profusion in so many parts of the Happy Valley.

CHAPTER X.

Road to Gulmarg—Barra Kountra—Babamirishi—The Gulmarg, or 'Mountain of Flowers'—European Visitors to Gulmarg—Log-houses—Their Construction—Their Advantages—Their Disadvantages—View of the Valley from Gulmarg—The Wet Season—Its Discomfort—Apathy of Hindu Servants—Life on the Marg—Our Church—Flowers and Ferns—Insect Life on the Marg—The Killan Marg—The Guluwans, or 'Horse-keepers;' Descendants of the Chákk Family—Their Habits and Mode of Life—Snakes in Kashmir—Effects of the Rarefied Air—Departure from Gulmarg—Road to Srinagar—The Zearat of a Rishi—The Rishis of Kashmir—Pattan—Conclusion of Tour in Western Part of Kashmir.

WE will now retrace our steps to Sopoor, in order to proceed to Gulmarg. After quitting this old and dilapidated town, an easy march of about eighteen miles brings us to the well-known and charming mountain retreat. Lying to the westward of Srinagar, Gulmarg may be reached by several routes; but the easiest, most convenient, and the prettiest, is the one we are now about to follow, having already in our wanderings arrived at the starting-point, which, if we were leaving the capital for the same ulterior destination, could be reached direct in twelve hours' journey by boat. The first stage on the road is from Sopoor to Barra Kountra, an easy march of between twelve and thirteen miles. The road is wide nearly all the distance, passing for some little way by the edge of the great lake, then by a village at the mouth of a valley formed of two 'kareewahs,' and then on to Naopore, which quitting, it ascends and crosses the natural alluvial deposit on the right, running into the pretty valley of the Ningil river, and, continuing along its right bank, brings us to our destination for the night, a village of some considerable size, situated on the hillside overlooking the vale we have lately traversed. The second stage is from Barra Kountra to the marg, a walk of only a little over five miles. The road, first turning to the left and passing through a gap, enters a narrow glen traversed by a small stream, and containing one or two small villages and farm-houses. Continuing up the glen the path leads to the foot of the mountains, and a steep and rough ascent of nearly a mile brings us to a place called Babamirishi, a small grassy plain on the top of the lower range of hills, deriving its name from the adjoining 'zearat' of a rishi, who, dying about four centuries ago, was here interred. His memory being held in extreme veneration by the Mohammedans, it is one of the most frequented places of this description in the whole of the Valley.

Leaving this holy site, the path leads up towards Gulmarg, distant a mile and a half, but fully one thousand feet higher up the mountain side. For the first half mile or so the ascent is steep and rough; but after that is surmounted a level stretch of about the same distance, through a grassy but narrow defile, leads us into the main valley, and, bearing to the left, another half mile shows us the usual encamping-ground of this favourite sanitarium, when the numerous tents and log-houses, that meet our gaze on our arrival, are evidences of the high estimation in which the flowery mountain is held as a place of residence by the yearly visitors to the Vale of Kashmir.

Gulmarg, or 'the mountain of flowers,' is a beautiful mountain common, a lovely spot on the downs of the Panjál, flat, green, and open, about two miles long, with a varying width from a few hundred yards to nearly a mile. On all sides it is bounded by hills, from which project numerous spurs in the form of grassy knolls, covered, as is also the whole surface of the marg, with flowers of every hue.

Hence its name 'gul,' a flower, and 'marg,' a mountain. The surrounding hills are densely clothed with forests of pine trees, and a small stream winding throughout its entire length lends life to the picture which, in the scenic disposition of its woods and glades, is rendered as highly picturesque as any spot in the Valley, partaking more, however, of the sylvan character of an English park than that of a natural formation on the summit of one of the lofty ridges of the Himalayas. Situated some 3000 feet above the level of Srinagar, the climate is cold, bracing, and salubrious; and although the rain falls pretty heavily at times, it is much preferred as a place of residence to the lower parts of the Valley and the capital during the hot and unhealthy months of July and August. At this season most of the European visitors to Kashmir, including the Resident and other officials, wend their way to the mountain retreat, which, unsought and unvisited for the greater portion of the year, becomes for a time the scene of that bustling activity, the natural characteristic of our countrymen and women, a large number of whom are here congregated together on a small space, and all leading a life of a free and gipsy-like character. Situated, as one may say, in the wilds, Gulmarg contains no houses or any other buildings of a permanent nature, and the only means open to the visitor to render himself comfortable and defy the weather is to dwell within the canvas walls of his tent, or build himself a wooden hut of a primitive and Crusoe-like character. Both these methods of housing oneself have their advocates, many preferring the tent, which, pitched upon the top of one of the knolls for the sake of dryness, is further rendered weather-proof by a framework of wood supporting a covering or roof of boughs, leaves, and earth, an ingenious contrivance which fairly answers the purpose for which it is intended. The majority, however, like a more stable habitation, one in which also a fire may be lighted, the evenings being sometimes cold and damp, particularly after a heavy storm. This is easily to be effected, for wood in any quantity is readily obtainable from the fallen trees in the surrounding forests, and a few rupees are sufficient to obtain the services of the native artizans who resort thither yearly, and gladly offer themselves as architects and builders. Very fair workmen they are. The result of their labour, which is completed in an incredibly short time, is a log hut, usually containing only one room. If rude in construction, it is dry and comfortable. The fire-place, built of stones and mud, answers its purpose very well, and, at the risk even of setting fire to your habitation, which happened in our case, is usually crammed full of wood, whose cheerful blaze is very acceptable, and not obtainable by the dwellers in tents, except out in the open air near the entrance of their abodes. The only weak spot in these temporary shelters is perhaps the roof, which always seems to leak in very stormy weather, and I have a lively recollection of the discomfort we endured, and the shifts and contrivances we employed to guard against this defect in our otherwise happy and comfortable home.

We paid our visit to Gulmarg in August, arriving there about the 6th. For the two first weeks following our arrival the rain poured down with hardly any intermission, a rather unusual occurrence in Kashmir, even in the wet season. We were so fortunate as to secure an empty hut the day we arrived, wet, cold, and hungry, after a long and wearisome march, owing to its proprietor and former occupier moving into a larger one he had erected on another spot. It was a well-built, single-roomed hut with an open verandah in front, and, standing as it did on the ridge directly overlooking the Valley, the whole expanse of the Vale lay spread out, a glorious panorama of mountains, meadows, forests, lakes, rivers, and canals, the rich foliage in many parts, and the waving fields of golden corn and rice, together with its villages and farm-houses, adding life to the scene nearer to us; while away in the distance the city of Srinagar was plainly discernible, with the two eminences close by of the Takt-i-Suliman and the Harri Parbut, which appeared, however, as mere ant-hills in comparison with the lofty and precipitous sides of the ridges that formed the background of the picture. In our humble dwelling-house we were snug enough, barring the little discomfort of the leakage through the roof, which sometimes even amounted to a perfect shower-bath during a heavy fall of rain, necessitating the employment of waterproofs and umbrellas to keep us dry. Under the shelter of these protections we sat during the day and slept at night, resigning ourselves with calmness to what appeared to be the inevitable; for despite all our attempts to render our habitation impervious to moisture by piling fresh branches and stamping down mud and earth on the roof, it still continued as leaky as an old sieve, the rain being too heavy and continuous for our puny efforts to restrain its percolation. As the only result obtained after all our exertions seemed to be the production of very muddy, instead of clear water, we let well alone, and waited patiently for better days. And these soon came; for gradually the storms were less frequent and lighter in character, and at the end of the two weeks ceased altogether, glorious weather following, which soon dissipated every memory of our former discomfort, and enabled us to enter upon the pleasant and careless existence followed by the dwellers on the 'marg,' our life on the mountain meadow being perhaps the most enjoyable time we spent during the whole of our stay in the Kashmirian Valley.

There was quite a colony of us collected here, with numerous natives and shopkeepers from the capital to supply our wants, a perfect bazaar being formed at one extremity of the 'marg.' This proved to be a downright godsend to the Hindu servants of the visitors, who daily gathered together to discuss the affairs of their masters and mistresses, and bewail their hard fate in leaving the sunny plains of their birth, for such a cold and uncongenial country and climate. Their love of gain is the only inducement that prompts them to this trial on their own part; for they possess no idea of the delights of travelling for travelling' sake, or to see new countries; and as for admiring the beautiful or the picturesque in nature, I could as readily imagine a monkey to be suddenly endowed with speech, and break into acclamations of joy, as a Hindu, or other inhabitant of India belonging to the class from whence servants are taken, to make any observation on the scenery, or to regard with any attention any unfamiliar tree or shrub, unless actuated by the hope of finding something edible growing upon its branches. But they love money; and for extra pay and a small subsistence allowance are willing to forsake for a time their beloved home, and wander, they know not where, in the train of their old sahib, or some other traveller in these regions, grumbling and complaining the whole time, but rarely deserting, the fear of losing their hardly-earned wage, and the expense they would incur for the return journey, being strong incentives to their remaining in a measure upon their good behaviour.

No matter in what country Englishmen are gathered together, there will be some variety of sport or pastime going forward. And in this respect we were not behind at Gulmarg; for a cricket and croquet-ground had been most artistically laid out on the green and level surface in the centre of the meadow, and a race-course, marked out with posts and rails, with sundry hurdles and artificial ditches, testified to the fact that the truly British sport of horse-racing was also at times followed out, although in a strange country, and far away from home. Our spiritual wants were not forgotten; for on the summit of a grass-covered mound was erected a small wooden church, primitive enough in appearance, but filled on Sundays with as devout a congregation as would be found in any nearer home, towards which our thoughts could scarcely fail to be directed, as the familiar words of our own simple but beautiful service fell upon the ear, while we worshipped our Maker, not as we had been accustomed to in stately edifices, but in a manner none the less earnest and devout, although offered up within the rough wooden walls of our temple in the wilderness.

Life flowed on most pleasantly at this charming spot, and we employed a good portion of our time each day in collecting and preserving various specimens of ferns and flowers, everywhere so abundant, many varieties of which, growing wild in rank profusion, were familiar to us as being cultivated with care and attention in our native country, while there were also many unknown. The whole surface of the 'marg' was one mass of blossom, yielding rich and rare treasures of the floral world to the enterprising botanist or collector. This place was also rich in insect life, more particularly in butterflies, for very few moths were met with; and having been from youth upward of an entomological turn of mind, a collection was formed, which is interesting as having afforded fifteen species found in England, as well as several varieties pretty abundantly distributed over other parts of Europe. There is a similar meadow about 1,000 feet above Gulmarg, called Killan, which, although somewhat longer and wider, is not nearly so pretty, but was interesting to us on account of its approach to the snow line, and affording other botanical specimens not to be met with lower down. It is about two and a half miles or so from Gulmarg, and can be reached by several paths leading through the fine dense pine forest upon its south-western side, the haunt of sundry bears and other animals, and apparently the favoured retreat of the 'guluwans' or horsekeepers, who tend the herds of cattle upon these mountain-downs, and whose roughly-built shanties or tattered tents were often met with on our road.

This curious race of people are the descendants of the old and warlike tribe of the Chákks, a family that in former days gave rulers and warriors to Kashmir, and who bravely resisted the invasion of their country by Akbar. In later times they have, however, only been remarkable for their predatory habits, and during the time of the Moguls and the Pathans they became formidable bands of brigands, infesting some of the principal roads in the country, making it dangerous for one to travel alone. They have rarely intermarried with any other caste; but they are few in number now; for at the beginning of this century, having made themselves so obnoxious by their murdering and plundering propensities, they were hunted down in their mountain retreats, and all who were left, in dread of the same fate, took to more peaceful avocations, their descendants, and the sole representatives of the great and powerful Chákks, being at the present day the dirty, half-starved, and fierce-looking men engaged in the mild and pastoral pursuit of tending droves of horses, sheep, and cows upon Gulmarg and similar places.

It was a pleasant walk up to Killan through the forest, in the damp and gloomy recesses of which many rare and beautiful ferns were to be found, and one could grope about amidst fallen trees, leaves, and rocks without the dread that accompanies any such acts in India of coming upon a cobra or some other lively snake. Snakes, indeed, are not unknown in the Valley, but they appear to be rather uncommon, except in particular places, on the northern side of the Valley, on account of their liking to sun themselves upon the bold bare rocks that everywhere protrude through the surface of the ground upon that side, whereas on the other aspects, more particularly on the southern, the soil is everywhere much thicker, and with much more vegetation. Certain it is that very few are met with; I only saw one the whole time of our journeyings, and that was a non-poisonous variety, much resembling in appearance the common snake at home. The boa or rock-snake is said to have been seen in Kashmir, and there is a very poisonous reptile found on rocky places on the eastern side of the Valley, about a yard long, with a very thick body, and an appearance altogether very repulsive. This, however, I can only state on the authority of others, never having met with an example, and never having even heard of any one who had seen a reptile answering to the foregoing description. The 'marg,' which lay immediately under a lofty ridge of the Pir Panjál, whose deeper gullies and ravines contain perpetual snow, was an interesting place, affording, as I have said, some rare plants, although vegetation was as a rule nothing like so luxuriant as on the common lower down. There were glaciers at different spots, and several streams of icy-cold water poured from the ravines in the mountain side at its upper end, formed from the melting of the snow in the crevices of the rocks, affording us the means of cooling our beverages at the time of the usual halt for tiffin. We experienced at this place some considerable difficulty in breathing, much more so than at Gulmarg, where many suffer great inconvenience from this cause, attributable of course to the rarefied condition of the atmosphere at the height we were standing, some 11,000 feet above the sea level.

Towards the end of August every one commences to make preparations for departure, it being then cool and pleasant in the lower parts of the Valley; and we will now follow their example, as we have yet to explore and describe the unvisited eastern portion of the country, which contains some remarkable ruins, springs, and other interesting objects. One can proceed to this part of the Valley from Gulmarg direct, by skirting the forests on the slopes of the Panjál and making for Shupiyan, and thence on to Nohan, Vernag, and Islamabad; but it is a tedious and uninteresting journey, no place of any interest being met with until our arrival at the first-named town, already visited on our road to

Srinagar from the plains of India. Such being the case, we once more proceed to the capital by another and more direct route, and, after arrival and a necessary halt to lay in stores or whatever is required, start off to the eastward, the inspection of which will complete our tour of the Valley of Kashmir. Leaving the 'marg' then, we make for the village of Pattan, some fourteen miles away, the road passing through Babamirishi, the same as followed on our journey thither.

Here there is to be seen, as already mentioned, the 'zearat' of a famous rishi, Baba Pyoomden, who died some four centuries ago. His shrine is one of the most venerated, as well as the richest, in the whole of the Valley. It has also a monastery attached to it, in which a few 'rishis' or monks reside; but this once-important class of Mohammedans are shorn now of much of their influence and importance, and the few that are to be met with appear to be simply guardians of the tomb of some former canonised saint of their order. In former days they were an important class, peculiar to Kashmir, something akin to the fakirs of Hindustan. Originally wanderers in the jungle, they became possessed in time, chiefly through the liberality of the Mogul emperors, of lands, and convents, or monasteries. For many years these Mohammedan ascetics were much looked up to by the other inhabitants of the Valley, and being pious and blameless men, doubtless effected some good; but they gradually lost their prestige after the decline of the Delhi emperors, since which time it is said no real rishi has existed in Kashmir.

Leaving this place, an easy road leads past the villages of Ajeebal, Khipore, and Chandesir, five miles from which stands Pattan, at the base of a large kareewah, which it is necessary to descend in order to gain the village. From Pattan to Srinagar is a distance of seventeen miles, over a fairly level road leading through the fields, and subsequently down the avenue of poplars near the entrance to the Sher Garhi, finally passing over the Ameeri Kadal, or first bridge, on to the usual encamping-ground, which we left some pages back for the tour of the western portion of the Happy Valley.

CHAPTER XI.

The Eastern Portion of Kashmir—Objects of Interest—Journey by Doongah—Pandritan—Temple at Pandritan—Town of Pampoor—The Saffron-grounds at Pampoor—Cultivation of the *Crocus sativus*—Saffron—Its Uses—Quantity grown in Valley—Mineral Springs—Shar—Ironworks in Kashmir—Ruins at Ladoo—Temple at Payech—Avantipore—Bijbehara—Junction of the Veshau River—Kanbal—Town of Islamabad—Its former Greatness—The Anat Nág—Sacred Trout—The Spring of Bawan—Its Legend—Caves of Bhomjoo—The Liddar Valley—Sacred Cave of Ambernath—Legend of the Cave—Road to the Cave—The Sheesha Nág—Description of the Cave—Pilgrimage to Ambernath—Hindu Ceremony at the Cave—Vigne's Description and Remarks.

THERE are many objects of interest to be seen in the eastern portion of Kashmir, such as the principal springs and sources of the Jhelam, the ruins at Martand, the old town of Islamabad, and some smaller valleys, as the Nowboog and Liddar. All these places are easily reached, and if one cares to undertake some rough and arduous marching a visit can be paid to the Wardwan, and the celebrated Cave of Ambernath. A considerable portion of this tour may be made by water, navigation of the river being feasible as far as Kambal, a good two days' journey by boat from Srinagar, embracing in its course many of the places to be inspected, which one can land and visit, the remainder being reached by easy marches from the last-named village. Quitting then our encamping-ground at the capital in the now familiar 'doongah,' the boat proceeds very slowly along the base of the mountains stretching out from the Throne of Solomon, the river at this spot making several very large curves in its course which rather impedes the work of towing the craft up-stream. After proceeding in a calm and leisurely manner thus for a couple of hours or so, we arrive at Pandritan, once a large and flourishing city, the capital of the province, but now, alas: through the insane act of one of its ancient rulers, a mere heap of ruins.

It is stated that at one time this city covered an extent of ground of nearly three miles, and contained some remarkable buildings, notably a shrine founded by Asoka, in which was kept a tooth of the great Buddha, the founder of the then popular religion, of which this monarch was one of the most strenuous upholders. Nothing is left of this once sacred place, and there is little to linger over or to recall the memories of former days; for with the exception of a small temple nothing escaped the devastation caused by the act of the King Abhimanyú, who in some fit of rage, or from some other cause not exactly known, is stated to have been the author of the destruction of this flourishing city by means of fire. This temple, pyramidal in shape, is built of stone, the roof being elaborately carved, and in architectural design is similar to that at Martand, the apparent type of all the most ancient buildings of this description in the Valley. It stands in the centre of a pond, encircled by a grove of willows, which prevents many from inspecting its interior. For a similar reason, other old temples in India and elsewhere are often difficult of access, the erection of these buildings in water having for its object the placing them under the protection of that race of deities, the 'nagas,' who dwell beneath its surface, and render them more holy by resting upon the sacred element.

Pursuing our course we arrive, after about eight hours' journey, although the distance by land from the capital is only eight miles, at the old but half-ruined town of Pampoor. The river, which has been flowing towards the north, at this part of its course takes a bold sweep eastwards, and the town, which is said to have been founded some thousand years ago, stands on the right or northern bank, on an open plain or down commanding a fine and extensive view of the Valley. A Hindu city, as its name denotes—Pampoor being a corruption of Padma-pur, the 'city of Vishnu'—in former days it was of considerable importance; but at present there is little to interest the stranger; for it contains but few houses, in nowise remarkable, an old mosque, in which some very fine woodwork is to be seen, being about the chief specimen of architecture worth visiting. The richest soil in the Valley is said to be at this place, and this fact has been taken advantage of through ages past for the cultivation of the *Crocus sativus*, the stamens of whose flowers, known as saffron, is a chief article of commerce in this country, yielding a large revenue to the government.

The saffron-grounds occupy a large space upon the plains around Pampoor, some ten or twelve miles in circumference it is said, and its cultivation is of remote antiquity. If any reliance is to be placed upon the wild statements in the works treating of the ancient history of the country, a very remote age may be attributed to the existence of this industry indeed; for therein it is stated that the soldiers of Alexander, during his invasion of the Valley, were lost in admiration at the sight of such extensive beds of a beautifully and delicately-tinted purple flower. Without going so far back in the world's history, there is no reason to doubt, however, that saffron has been, as is now the case, most extensively cultivated in this part of the province, giving employment to a large number of people, who in the picking season are zealously watched by Sepoys, to prevent their appropriation of this valuable commodity. The plants, which are arranged in parterres after careful ploughing and preparation of the ground has been made, flower in October, and are then plucked, and their different coloured stamens picked out and separated. The red and white stamens only are of value, the yellow being generally given to the cattle. The former, however, after proper preparation, yield that principal ingredient of Oriental cooking, the well-known dye-stuff, and the article called saffron employed in medicine, the yearly exports of which from Kashmir to India amount in value to the sum of twenty thousand rupees. This is a small amount to what no doubt was exported in former days, for a large portion of the supply in ancient times was yielded by this country; but the demand also has fallen off; and as its medicinal value has long been declining, very little is needed in Europe for the uses to which it is now applied—the flavouring and colouring confectionary and other articles of food. It is a curious fact in relation to this subject that in that division of our own country called Cornwall saffron has always been, and is still, largely used in several articles of diet as a flavouring and colouring principle, and I am given to understand that its employment has been known there from time immemorial. As this article is one of the principal ingredients in the preparation of the various articles of food consumed in the different countries of Asia, more particularly in India and the central parts of that quarter of the globe, might not its general use, like a custom handed down from their forbears in this part of England, be accepted as a further proof of the supposed direct Asiatic origin of the Cornish people, connecting their race with the first swarm of the primitive Aryan stock on their migration to Europe, which subsequently became almost entirely colonized by the successive streams that poured down from the mother nation on that part of the Iranian plateau near the Hindu Koosh?

From Pampoor several small excursions may be made, notably to the mineral springs at Weean, the iron mines a little further on, and the ruins at Ladoo. The first-named is a small village, some three miles to the north-east, and near it are three mineral springs, highly impregnated with iron and sulphur, and which in their medicinal virtues would be a source of great attraction to invalids, and make the fortune of any place, if only situated in some more accessible region.

Two miles south-east from here is the village of Shar, at the back of which is a lofty range of mountains, containing the ore from which most of the iron manufactured in the Valley is smelted, in a rude and primitive fashion. Ironworks also exist at Soap, some little distance off, and veins of lead, copper, silver, and gold are known to exist in the hills of the Valley, only waiting for the experienced hand of a Cornish miner to rifle their rich and rare treasures. Failing this I much fear they will never see the light; for in all these years, although perfectly aware of the existence of such mineral wealth, the inhabitants of Kashmir have never made any attempt to ascertain their extent, or work them in any way—iron, and that of bad and indifferent quality, being the only metal as yet produced at their hands.

The ruins at Ladoo, which consist of an old temple standing in a tank, are about a mile from

Shar, but need not detain us; so making our way back to Pampoor, we take to the boat again, and a four hours' pull brings us to Karkarpore, where a halt must be made to visit the temple at Páyech, the most beautifully proportioned of all the old buildings in Kashmir. This exquisite little building, one of the latest and most interesting of the old Hindu age, is about six miles off the halting-place, and is very easily reached, the road being fairly good all the way. Being dedicated to Vishnu as Suryea, or the 'sun god,' the ceiling is radiated so as to represent that orb, small sitting figures of the popular preserver of the universe being inserted in niches on the cornice outside. Though small, being only nine feet square and about six feet high, it is, both in its exterior and interior, particularly elegant, and well deserves a visit. It is also in good preservation, despite the attempts of the Pathans, when the Valley was under their rule, to take it down and remove it, doubtless as an ornament, to the capital.

Some little distance further up the river, and on its right bank, a large ruined city next attracts our attention, one of the former capitals of the province during the Hindu *regime*, and called Avantipore, after the King Avante Verma, its reputed founder.

It was a flourishing place in the days of yore; but being deserted for Srinagar, its temples and other buildings, most probably overthrown by the Mohammedans, fell into decay, and are only to be traced by the heaps of fallen materials and the stonework that formed their base. A long stretch of water, to cover which takes nearly ten hours, the rapidity of the current only allowing a mile or so to be made in an hour, brings us to a part of the Jhelam very wide and deep, and spanned by a bridge. On the left bank stands the large but somewhat dilapidated town of Bijbehara; nothing remarkable being passed on the journey excepting the junction of the Veshau, one of the largest rivers in the country, with the stream we are now floating on, which takes place some three miles below this ancient city.

The town of Bijbehara is not very interesting, all the houses bearing somewhat the aspect of decay. Neither is the place itself or the country around what might be called in any way picturesque, for the locality is bare of trees, excepting on the southern side of the river, where a fine grove of chenars stands, denoting the former site of a once flourishing garden. At one time a very fine temple, built by Asoka, B.C. 250, stood on this spot, but it was pulled

To face page 243

From a photograph by Mr. H. Simpson. Stanford's Geog. Estab.

ISLAMABAD FROM THE HILL ABOVE

down during the reign of Sikander; and the curious in these matters may obtain a sight of another fine old example of these buildings erected on the top of the Samma Thang, that curious conical hill, the same on which Kashuf is stated to have lived for several centuries in pious meditation, preparing for his great act of draining the Valley, the mound being within a short distance of the town.

Kanbal, our present destination, is now only some four miles by land, the journey by boat up the gradually narrowing river occupying, however, four hours. This is the termination of our water trip, the further continuation of the tour having to be made by land. The first stage is Islamabad, a very short distance off, the starting-point to many places of interest within easy reach, as well as several further away.

Islamabad, the ancient Anat Nág, 'the spring of Anat,' the serpent of Vishnu, and the emblem of eternity, but now known only by its present designation, which signifies 'the abode of the Mohammedan faith' was once the largest town in Kashmir, the capital alone excepted. To the traveller of to-day it presents, however, but a shadow of its former greatness and prosperity, the few houses that are left, some of which are highly ornamented with the trellis and lattice-work peculiar to the country, appearing half-ruined and neglected, affording a speaking evidence of the past and present condition of the town, its light and joyous prosperity having fled the place long since. The rapacity of its Pathan and Sikh governors was the means of conducing to this dire result. The town is situated about a mile from the right bank of the Jhelam, on the westward of and close under an elevated 'kareewah,' the largest of these curious table-lands, being six miles long, and as many broad, and from the foot of which several springs issue; the principal, the Anat Nág, being close by a pleasure garden called the Sirkari Bagh. This holy fountain issues from the foot of the hill, and flows through a series of canals and tanks, built up with stone, to the outside of an enclosure formed by a huge wall surrounding the site, where the waters then fall to the ground in the form of a cascade of considerable size. All the tanks and canals are filled with trout, and being considered by the Hindus as sacred, they are bountifully fed by the pious worshippers at the fount, in consequence of which they become very tame, and attain to goodly proportions. Many similar springs exist near this spot, the waters of one or two of them being conducted to the town by aqueducts for useful purposes. One that issues from a fissure in the rock is highly sulphureous and slightly warm, possessing without doubt active medicinal properties.

Some five miles away from Islamabad, by the direct road on the northern side of the 'kareewah,' is to be seen a spring, a very sacred spring, the most holy perhaps in the country, near a small village called Bawan, a name derived from the water, which, gushing from a fissure in the limestone rock, the base of the raised plain of alluvium intervening between the town and the mountains beyond, is known as, or is called *par excellence*, Bawan, 'The Spring.' Its origin is of course fabulous, being considered due to the act of Kashuf, who, walking about in intense enjoyment on the dry land, the result of his great achievement now completed, saw an egg, the supposed mundane egg of the Hindus, lying on the ground. Attracted by its glittering appearance he picked it up, but being of a brittle disposition it broke in his hand; and from the spot on which the pieces fell forthwith flowed the spring, which, dedicated to Vishnu, is now, as it has been for ages past, a standing evidence of the credulity of the mild Hindu, numbers of whom, on account of its divine origin, yearly visit its source to gain forgiveness for their sins, and happiness in the next world. It is a very similar spring to the one already described, and like it the water is conveyed away through a series of tanks and canals swarming with Himalayan trout, fed and protected by the priests, who dwell on the spot, deriving a living from the pecuniary offerings of the pious and curious that come within their reach, to whom they do the honours of the place, having an eye to the backsheesh in the manner characterizing the members of this class of native society. The caves of Bhoomjoo, places of pilgrimage, can hence be easily visited, being distant only about a mile, and in the mountains bounding the right side of the road that leads up the Liddar Valley. There are several of these caverns, the two largest of which are called respectively the 'Long Cave, and the 'Temple Cave,' the first-named being traversable for seventy yards, but penetrating very much further into the rock, the natives believing it to be interminable. The other is not nearly so long, but is higher and wider, and contains a very well-built Hindu temple, about twelve feet square, a fine specimen of architecture, whence its name, the Temple Cave, is derived. From here an expedition may be made up the Liddar Valley, which, opening into this, the north-eastern corner of Kashmir, and giving passage to a river of the same name, extends for a distance of twenty-five miles to just beyond Palgam, where, narrowing, it separates into two defiles, one of which leads into the Sind Valley, already visited, the other bringing one by toilsome marches to the Sheesha Nág, and the sacred cave of Umur, or Ambernath.

We did not visit this cave, the distance, and the roughness, and sometimes even—owing to landslips—the dangerous condition, of the road deterring us from undertaking such a journey; but as a spot of great interest, and annually visited by thousands of pilgrims, it may not be out of place to give a short description of this holy spot, and the origin of its sanctity, as told to Vigne by a native of the country, that traveller himself having been prevented by weather and other causes from reaching the place itself. As regards the origin of the name, 'Umur' signifies 'the immortal,' and 'Nath' is a Sanscrit word applied to the principal Hindu divinities, as lords and masters, chiefly to Vishnu, and occasionally to Siva, and also to the place where they are worshipped and supposed more particularly to reside; the name prefixed being sometimes that of the place where they are worshipped, sometimes that of the builder of the shrine. In this case it is a place of pilgrimage sacred to Siva, who is supposed to reside within the cavern in the form of a block of ice; and the legend of its sanctified origin runs as follows:

"The angel of death appeared to the divinities, and told them that he would destroy them. They were much troubled at this threat, and proceeded to the place of abode of the Lord Siva, and entreated his protection. Siva appeared to them with a bright and pleasing countenance, and showing them great favour, inquired into their state and circumstances with much anxiety. The divinities represented that the angel of death was at enmity with them, and that they dreaded his power. Upon which Siva, of his great mercy and kindness, bestowed upon them the water of immortality, by which they were freed from the persecution of the angel of death. Siva afterwards again went to his devotional abstractions at his abode, and was again sought for by the divinities; but they could not see him. They were therefore in great distress, and lifted up their hands in prayer, and intreated him to show himself to them, whence the pilgrimage and prayer at the cave of Ambernath."

Being to the Hindus what Mecca is to the Mohammedans, it is annually resorted to for the ceremony which takes place there, on or about the 28th of July of each year, before which date crowds of pilgrims, of every rank and caste, from every part of Kashmir and Hindustan, collect together at Islamabad, and march to the cave by stages up the Liddar Valley as far as Palgam, and then prosecute their journey, which now becomes rough and perilous, up the defile leading north-east, which brings them to their destination. As far as Palgam, distant twenty-six miles, the road is fairly easy; but on leaving the main valley and entering the defile on the right, the path, though worn by the pilgrimages of ages, is rocky and fatiguing, and rendered often dangerous by landslips or avalanches, causing frequent fatal accidents. The victims are, however, scarcely mourned for by their relatives, their death in the performance of a pious act rendering them meet for a happy future. Some fifteen miles up the defile the Sheesha Nág, 'the glassy' or 'leaden lake,' is reached, from which the incipient Liddar river flows, a small sheet of water about a third of a mile in diameter, lying in a punch-bowl formed by the nearly perpendicular precipices of a limestone ridge, as much twisted and distorted as the same formation on other parts of the hills rising from the plain of Kashmir, having most probably been formed at the same period. Fourteen miles further on the cave itself is reached, which, situated on the snowy mountains at an altitude of 16,000 feet, is a desolate and weird spot, the surrounding scenery being described by those who have seen it as of Titanic splendour. The cave is of gypsum, about fifty yards long by nearly the same breadth, with a height of about thirty feet, and contains, it is said, stalactites, icicles, and large blocks of ice in the clefts of the rocks, which are most probably frozen springs. The ceremony that takes place on the arrival of the pilgrims is thus described:*

"A vast multitude of men, women, and children advance towards the cave, at an hour appointed by the attendant, the Brahmans first divesting themselves of all clothing, excepting some pieces of birch bark. When the pilgrims arrive at its mouth they commence shouting, clapping their hands, and calling upon Siva. 'Show yourself to us,' is the universal and simultaneous exclamation and prayer of prostrate thousands. The cave is much frequented by rock-pigeons, which, affrighted by the noise, rush out tumultuously, and are the answer to the prayer. In the body of one or other of these

* VIGNE, *Travels in Kashmir*, vol. ii.

resides the person of their divinity; and Siva, the Destroyer and the All-powerful, is considered to be present, and incarnate as the harmless dove. If there happens to be no pigeon in the cave at the time, the pilgrims are much disappointed, although I could not learn that they augured anything particularly bad from its non-appearance. The Fakirs and Brahmans at all events make a good thing of it; their maintenance is an inculcated duty, and they grow comparatively rich by the presents they receive during the expedition."

Regarding the origin and reason for this ceremony, the same author further observes: "The dove, as need scarcely be remarked, has often figured as a metaphor and as a tenement and receptacle for divinity, both in sacred and profane history, the same bird having been even called upon by the Musulmans to dispense with its natural timidity in aid of their prophet, and to build its nest in the cave where Mahomet took refuge upon his flight from Mecca. The analogy may, perhaps, have been accidental; and although the account of the pilgrimage as detailed above be redolent with ignorance, superstition, and priestcraft, yet at the same time one cannot help thinking of the dove of the ark, and of the wilderness, and of our own sacred writings. The dove has always been the emblem of peace; the sublime and the preternatural have always been the concomitants of the wilderness; solitude accompanied by any extraordinary degree of remoteness has often been a cause of sanctification, and the more wild and gloomy the locality, the better has it been thought qualified to become the peculiar residence of a god. But surely such a custom as is here detailed, and which in all probability must have existed for ages before the coming of Christ, is not to be looked upon in the light of a mere augury from the flight of birds, or an attempt to find out whether Siva be or not propitious, by his deigning to be present or absent as a dove in its natural habitation. A thinking and unprejudiced mind would rather be induced to consider whether it were not, partly at least, founded on some original revelation made to the inhabitants of this earth by their Creator, and to recognise in the whole account no powerless addition to the numerous presages of incarnation and redemption, corroborative of the Mosaic records, which have been noticed by all writers on the religion of the Hindus as dimly distinct amongst the dark confusion and anachronisms of its own recorded history."

CHAPTER XII.

The Ruins of Martand—Temple of the Sun—Its Antiquity—The Pandus—Vigne's Description of the Architecture of the Temple—Its Exterior—Its Interior—Effects of Earthquakes—Peculiarities observed in the Architecture of old Ruins in Kashmir—Vigne's Opinion—The Wardwan Valley—The Springs of Kashmir—The Atchibal Spring—The Bringh River—Identity of River and Spring—Bernier's Description of Atchibal—The Water of the Spring—The Vernag Spring—Road to Vernag—Shangus—Dancing Girls of Shangus—The Nowboog Valley—The Tansan Bridge—The Kookar Nág—The Shahabad Valley—The Spring of Vernag—Source of the Jhelam—The Garden of the Spring—The Mogul Emperor Jehangir—Nur Mehal, the Light of the Palace—Her Parentage—The Rozloo Valley—The Veshau River—Its Source—The Konsa Nág—Cataract of Haribal—Road to Shupiyan—End of Tour—Concluding Remarks.

OF all the interesting sights in the vicinity of Islamabad the ruins of Martand hold the first place, and they are easy of access, being situated only five miles from the city, on the highest part of the kareewah, where it commences to rise to its junction with the mountains. This old Hindu temple, originally dedicated to the worship of the sun, and called Pandu Koru by the natives of the Valley, is now only a ruin, but enough yet remains to enable one to form a fair opinion of what it must have been in early days, when a leading specimen of a gigantic style of architecture. Although not able to boast of an equality with that well-known example at Palmyra, or the remains of the palace at Persepolis, yet it deserves to be ranked with them, and in situation on a natural platform at the foot of some of the noblest mountains in the world is far superior to either. Nothing is known with any certainty as to its antiquity, its founders, or its original use; but as the greater part of the old ruins in Kashmir were built between the time of Asoka and the reign of Avante Verma, that would give us from B.C. 250 to A.D. 875, a wide range of years, during which numerous temples and other edifices were erected in the Valley, the same style being apparent in all of them, even down to the building already noticed at Páyech, the most modern of all, erected some considerable time after the one now under consideration, which, according to the best authorities, was built between the fifth and sixth centuries of the Christian era. The natives of the country, however, attribute to it a much greater antiquity, as its name denotes—Pandu Koru signifying 'the house of the Pandus,' the sons of Pand, a monarch of the Lunar race of ancient

To face page 254.

From a photograph by Mr H. Simpson.

Stanford's Geog[l] Estab[t].

THE RUINS OF MARTAND.

Hindu kings, who, driven from India, in the course of their wanderings visited Kashmir, and erected numerous temples, notably the temple of Martand. This kind of legend, however, applies to every old building in the East of whose origin there exists no reliable information, all being considered by the Hindus the work of these princes or their immediate descendants. In the book before mentioned a very good descriptive account of this temple and its style of architecture is given, together with the opinion of other authorities on the subject, which is well worth perusal, and to which I am indebted for the following abridged account.*

At present all that remains of the Temple of Martand consists of a central and rectangular building, surrounded by a court or quadrangle and rectangular colonnade facing inwards, the length of the outer side of the wall being about ninety yards, and that of the front about fifty-six. The remains of three gateways opening into the court, the principal fronting due east towards Islamabad, are still standing. It is also rectangular in its details, and built with enormous blocks of limestone of many feet in length, and of proportionate solidity, and all cemented with an excellent mortar.

VIGNE'S *Travels in Kashmir*, vol. i. p. 385.

Several of the pillars of the colonnade are still standing, and between each are trefoiled niches; while the capitals of the larger pillars are richly carved and ornamented, their shafts, which are grooved rather than fluted, being also surmounted by an ornamented neck of beads. The façade of the building which stands in the interior is abreast of the gates of either colonnade, and one-third of the whole length of the quadrangle intervenes between it and the front gate, which faces to the west, a bank of stones and rubbish occupying the place where there was originally a flight of steps leading to the doorway. Both sides of the doorway on the front are carved in relievos, being miniature representations of those in the interior; but they are so much injured by time as to be scarcely perceptible, excepting when the sun brings them out with a strong shadow. The interior is divided into two compartments; that at the entrance is nine yards in length, and at the western end is an inner chamber or crypt five yards long, surrounded by blank walls, but open like the other to the face of day, all semblance of a roof having long since disappeared beneath the shocks of earthquakes and the unsparing hand of Sikunder But-Shikan.

In the centre of either side of the larger anterior

chamber is a window reaching to the floor, and about eight feet in height. The walls, thus divided quarterly, are filled up with single figures in relief, two of Surya, and two of Luchmi, one in each panel. The building was once apparently two stories high, and, judging from other ruins in the country, the upper part was certainly pyramidal, and the whole fabric must have been of considerable height; for its present height, of forty feet or so, has been diminished by earthquakes even within the memory of man, and at the time Vigne visited it, some forty years ago, he was assured by an intelligent native, that he himself remembered it much higher. Perhaps the only unaccountable parts of the ruins are two side buildings, like detached wings, sculptured with figures of the same character as those inside the building; but most probably these were merely ornamental, and joined by a flying buttress to the upper part of the centre building.

Details characteristic of different styles are observable in the architecture of this temple, and that part of the subject is treated of by the same author, who mentions also that he was struck with the great general resemblance which it bore to the recorded disposition of the ark and its surrounding curtains, in imitation of which the temple at Jerusalem was built. The general conclusions, however, arrived at were, that Kashmir, having been, from its insulated situation, its climate, and other advantages, a place of consequence from the very earliest ages, it is probable that its architecture, or some of its peculiarities, like that of Egypt, is more likely to have afforded a prototype than to be a copy of any known style, while it seems indeed to be peculiar to the Valley; for there is nothing exactly like it in Hindustan, or in any country to the westward of the Indus. One great authority on ancient architecture has stated that the temples in Kashmir, all of which bear a strong resemblance as to their manner of construction, are decidedly separated in style from all known examples; but as the chief points of difference between these buildings and the Roman are of a Hindu character, infers that their builders were Hindu imitators of the Roman rather than Roman or Grecian imitators of the Hindu, seeing that the forms approach or imitate the Roman, whereas the workmanship is of the former character—the Parthian conquests in Syria giving an opportunity to the Eastern workmen to see the buildings of that country, and even of Egypt, by which new forms were suggested. This agrees very well with the date usually assigned to them, namely, between 250 B.C. and 875 A.D. There are a great number of these buildings in the Valley, but Martand is the principal, although not the earliest example. All, however, are nearly similar in architectural design, as described above, a fact that cannot fail to be noticed by those who have inspected the curious building at Pandritan, the edifice at Páyech, the erection on the summit of the Takt-i-Suliman, which have been described in these pages, and which, with the addition of the ruins to be seen in the Báramúla Pass, and the Temple of the Sun, so lately under consideration, are the chief types of native architecture in the Valley, and should be visited and studied by all tourists as emblems of the former prosperity of a country which they could not do otherwise than have adorned.

The Wardwan Valley may be reached by four marches from Islamabad, but it is rarely visited, except by the sportsman, who will there, if he is fortunate, meet with ibex and other game, which may repay him in a measure for the cold and damp climate of this rugged region, and the rough life incidental to his pursuit. It is a long and narrow valley of about forty miles in length, with a breadth only on an average of a quarter of a mile, bounded on either side by high and rugged mountains—one very lofty range separating it from the main Valley of Kashmir. A river of the same name traverses its length, and there are a few thinly-inhabited villages or scattered huts, but nothing to interest the stranger, or call forth a visit, save for the purpose mentioned above, for which it is greatly famed.

In addition to its rivers and lakes, the country of Kashmir has long been celebrated for its magnificent springs, some of which we have already visited. They are, however, small in comparison with the two towards which we now direct our steps. The first and largest is that of Atchibal, situated some six miles to the east of Islamabad, at the foot of a low range of hills, the water rising from beneath the limestone rock that forms the extremity of the spur. It gushes out in several places, but the principal spring makes its way up through a large fissure, with force sufficient to throw a stream of water some considerable height above the level of its margin—a fact apparently indicating a descent from the lofty mountains behind it, rather than the generally accepted theory that it is only the reappearance of a river called the Bringh, which, a few miles away, after flowing for some little distance, suddenly disappears through the bottom of a large fissure in its stony bed.

This theory of the identity of the river and spring has long been credited by the natives of the Valley, and it is most probably correct; for the direction thus ascribed to the river is much the same that it would have followed on the surface; and it has been also stated that small pieces of wood or other articles thrown into the Bringh above the place of its disappearance have reappeared at Atchibal, a full proof of the existence of a large subterraneous passage. Many years ago this spring was a favourite resort, not only of the old kings of Kashmir, but also of their successors, the Great Moguls; and it must have been a pleasant spot in the time of Bernier, the first European who ever visited the Valley, about the year 1663, and who, in his *Travels in India*, a series of letters in French concerning his journey to Kashmir, in Aurungzebe's suite, writes of it thus: "In returning from Send Brary I turned a little out of the highway, in order to sleep at Archiavel (Atchibal), which is a place of pleasure belonging to the old kings of Kashmir, and at present to the Great Mogul. Its principal beauty is a fountain, of which the water disperses itself on all sides around a building which is not devoid of elegance, and flows through the gardens by a hundred canals. It comes out of the earth as if it remounted and returned from the bottom of a well with violence and boiling, and in such abundance that it may rather be called a river than a fountain. Its water is admirably good, and is so cold that to hold the hand within it could scarcely be borne. The garden is very beautiful on account of its alleys, the great quantity of fruit-trees, apricots, and cherries, the quantity of *jets-d'eau* of all kinds of figures, of reservoirs full of fish, and a kind of cascade very high, which in falling makes a great sheet of thirty or forty paces in length, the effect of which is admirable, particularly at night, when they have placed below it an infinity of little lamps, which are arranged in holes made on purpose in the well, all which is of very great beauty."

A great alteration has taken place since the time when this was written; for although the building, the reservoir, and the garden mentioned by Bernier, all of which were constructed by Shah Jehan, are still standing, they are in ruins, overshadowed by the large chenar trees that, probably planted at the same time, have, left to themselves, continued to grow and increase in size and beauty. Whilst the work of man's hand has, like everything else in Kashmir, fallen to decay, Nature's handiwork remains the same. The magnificent stream flows on as in days of yore; and the waters of the different sources, uniting soon after leaving the garden, form a small river, which, flowing peacefully on for some little distance, eventually joins the Jhelam near the town of Islamabad.

The other large spring is that of Vernag, distant some fifteen miles away from Atchibal, the road lying along the plains, and comparatively easy to travel. But there is also another which we will take, as it will allow of our visiting the Nowboog Valley, and a collection of springs called the Kookar Nág. whose waters are very cold, and celebrated throughout the country for their purity. Pursuing this road we turn eastwards, after leaving Atchibal, and soon arrive at an old tumble-down village called Shangus, celebrated in former days as containing a colony of nautch girls, famous for their beauty and talent, but who possess no representatives at the present time on this spot, the family having apparently died out or emigrated to some other locality. A mile or so further on is another small village, close to the commencement of the long, narrow pass, through which the path leads to the

Nowboog valley, a small but beautiful glen of about eight miles long, bounded by pine-clad mountains on either side, abounding with bears and other animals; and as, from its situation, the climate is agreeable, it is often the resort of sportsmen and others, attracted thither by the charm of its scenery, the ground being park-like and covered with low and swelling hills, carpeted with rich grass, and sufficiently interspersed with streams and patches of forest to be rendered exceedingly picturesque, and a delightful spot for the lovers of Nature.

Leaving the Valley, the road, turning to the right, brings us after seven miles or so of easy marching to the Tansan bridge, thrown over the river Bringh, crossing which we find ourselves on the highway from Kashmir to Kishtwar.

This bridge, near which stands on the hillside the Musjid of Hajee Daud Sahib, is a place of some strength and strategical importance, and has been the scene of many a struggle in former days, between the Kashmiris and the inhabitants of Kishtwar, being the key to the possession of the Bringh Valley, which debouches on the plain immediately opposite. Numerous were the fights at this spot during the feuds that prevailed amongst the people of these two mountainous countries before the latter territory was finally invaded by Gulab Singh, and the last of its independent rajahs, Teg Singh, giving himself up without fighting, it became a part of the Jamoo and Kashmir possessions. Five miles to the north-west of this bridge is the Kookar Nág, a beautiful spring, gushing out most copiously in several places from the foot of the limestone rock, which forms the base of a long range of verdant hills separating the 'pergunnah' of Bringh from that of Shahabad. On the other side of the range lies the Shahabad valley, which contains what was once the town of that name, the largest at this end of the province, but now dwindled down to the mere dimensions of a village; and some three miles further, we come to the spring of Vernag, the most celebrated of all the numerous springs in Kashmir, and undoubtedly the principal source of the river Jhelam.

This famous spring is on the opposite side of the strath from Shahabad, and close under the mountains bordering this end of the Valley, a range which is crossed by the traveller proceeding by the Jummoo and Banihal route, the pass of that name being entered within a short distance of the fountain. The water, which is very cold, gushes out in considerable volume, being at first received into an octagonal stone basin, nearly forty yards wide, and of great depth, and filled with sacred trout. On leaving this basin, it flows through the garden in a series of canals, passing out as a considerable stream. Shortly, joining the Sandrahan river, it rolls steadily onwards to develop further on into the broad deep Jhelam, the principal river of Kashmir, which, commencing near Islamabad by the junction of the Arpat, Bringh, and Sandrahan (three streams owing their origin chiefly to the several springs we have visited), is navigable nearly from its beginning, and, possessing a channel sufficient for carrying off the rain and snow from the mountains that surround the Valley, is one of its principal beauties, and no less important a factor in the prosperity of the country which it so materially adorns.

Around the spring are the ruins of an old garden and palace, built about the year 1619, by the Emperor Jehangir, and his lovely consort, on which account only are they interesting. It is stated that this place was the favourite spot above all others in the country with that monarch, who, taken ill at Baramgalla on his road to Kashmir, expressed a wish to be transported thither that he might die beside the spring he loved so well, and had so much adorned—the magnificent basin that receives the water being also mainly formed under his direction. However, he was not to see it again; for his decease took place before his orders could be obeyed, and his body was removed to Lahore. when a magnificent mausoleum still stands, erected in loving memory by the dear companion of his travels and residence in the Happy Valley, during the thirteen visits he paid to that favoured portion of the dominions that acknowledged him as master.

Of all the Great Moguls, the name of Jehangir is perhaps the most renowned in the Valley, and equally so is that of his wife Nur Mahal, to whom is due the designs of tne numerous buildings, fountains, and gardens erected during the lifetime of her august consort, the ruined remains of which have been noticed and described at various parts of our tour. The Kashmirians still reverence her name, and even claim her as a countrywoman, asserting that she was a native of the Valley, but cannot adduce any facts in support of this assertion, or disapprove the more authentic story of her birth found in Indian history, which proves her to be the daughter of the Persian adventurer Itmad-ood-Dowlah, whose tomb at Agra is one of the interesting sights of that city.

Eight miles from Vernag is the pretty little valley of Rozloo, oval in shape and three miles long by two broad. It is a fertile spot, bounded on the south by the grassy slopes of the Pir Panjál, containing several villages, and much frequented by visitors in search of the picturesque. As we have now pretty well exhausted the chief places of interest in this portion of Kashmir, we may return to the capital by way of Islamabad, or continue along the southern side of the Valley, and on to Shupiyan, visiting *en route* the cataract at the source of the Veshau, which brings us to the termination of the entire tour of the province, and to the town where we halted on our road to Srinagar, by the Pir Panjál route, and where we made our entrance into the country we had come to visit.

The town of Shupiyan is some thirty miles from our last halting-place, the Rozloo Valley. The road, skirting the foot of the hills for the first part of the way, and then opening into the plains, passes by the villages of Ban Doosar and Nohan, the two usual resting-places for the night on this march of twenty miles. From the latter place, the road soon opens into a fine grassy plain, and then continues along the left bank of the river Veshau, to the mouth of the gorge through which it issues from the mountains. This fine river, the largest in Kashmir, the Jhelam alone excepted, rises from the Konsa Nág, a far-famed lake, a noble mountain tarn, situated on the very top of the Pir Panjál, at an elevation of between twelve and thirteen thousand feet. The lake itself, according to the observations of other travellers, for I did not attempt the arduous march to the summit of the mountain ridge upon which it is situated, is nearly a mile in length, with a breadth of five hundred to six hundred yards, and of some considerable depth. At the eastern end, the banks slope gently downwards to the water's edge, but on the northern and southern sides, the bare rock rises very abruptly from the water to a height of 1,400 feet, with remarkably pointed peaks and bare scarped sides. The fresh and unworn appearance of the eastern side, forbids the idea that this extraordinary place has ever been the crater of a volcano, which the more irregular and heaped-up appearance of the western bank might otherwise have tended to encourage. From these facts it has been inferred that the cavity was formed by the sinking of the lower, and of the tabular rocks on the eastern bank, and that the northern bank or dam remains more rounded in consequence of its not having been sufficiently a sharer in the force which has upraised the other, the valley of the lake having been most probably formed by the forcible separation of the mountain-top. Leaving the lake through an irregular rocky opening in its western side, the water of the river Veshau falls into a deep and picturesque channel, which it has worn for itself in the bare rock. Here there are several ledges, over which it dashes, forming cataracts or waterfalls. The largest of these is Haribal, undoubtedly the finest cataract in Kashmir, which can be viewed perfectly by ascending a steep path on the left of the road at the entrance of the gorge. This leads to a lofty rock overhanging the torrent, about a quarter of a mile from where it debouches into the plains. Pursuing a south-easterly direction, from a wide-spreading and fordable stream it becomes a deep unfordable river of considerable width, some little distance from its junction with the Jhelam, five miles below the town of Bijhehara.

After viewing the fall, a place of peculiar sanctity with the Hindus, we continue our march to our destination; and passing through a very pretty village called Sedau, about a mile from the Veshau gorge, an easy walk of another five miles brings us to Shupiyan, the termination of the march, and also of our tour.

Hence one can proceed back to the capital by Ramoo and Chrar, on the road already described, particularly if the return journey to India is to be made by the Marri route. This proceeding, however, is totally unnecessary if the Imperial road is to be selected, for which Shupiyan forms a good starting-point, supplies of all kinds being usually abundant. But the choice of roads may be safely left to the discretion of the traveller, and I need not say more. My task is finished, and my promise fulfilled of indicating the roads to Kashmir, describing the chief places of interest in the Happy Valley, and the manners and customs of its inhabitants—as far as I am able in the scope of the present volume. Should any remarks or information conveyed here have proved of interest to those who peruse these pages, or should they in the future serve as some little guide and assistance to intending travellers in the romantic Vale, I shall deem myself amply repaid by the knowledge that my work has been of some service, and can only beg of my readers to deal leniently with any shortcomings they may find.

APPENDIX I.

ROUTE NO. 1.

The Gújerát and Pir Panjál Route.

No.	NAME.	DISTANCE.	REMARKS.
	Gújerát to—		
1	Dowlatnagar .		The first three stages are usually accomplished in one journey, either by stage-cart or dhooly-dâk. Road fairly good to Bhimber.
2	Kotla . . .		
3	Bhimber . .	28½ miles	
4	Saidabad . .	15 "	Road fairly good. Several rivers have to be forded, and Aditak range crossed. Good bungalow.
5	Naoshera . .	12½ "	Range of Kaman Goshi has to be crossed, and stream forded several times; from foot of pass fair road. Good bungalow; supplies abundant.
6	Changas	13½ "	Road along valley of Tawi. Fairly easy travelling through very fine scenery. Good bungalow.

The Gújerát and Pir Panjál Route (continued).

No.	Name.	Distance.	Remarks.
	Changas to—		
7	Rajaori . .	14 miles	Easy road along valley of Tawi, which river has to be forded near the town, the largest met with on the journey. An open pavilion in garden serves as a rest bungalow. Good encamping ground.
8	Thanna Mundi	14 ,,	Easy road, still along valley of Tawi. Fair bungalow.
9	Baramgalla .	10½ ,,	The Rutten Pir, 8,200 feet high, has to be crossed. Rather rough travelling at first; from foot of pass fairly easy road to village. Bungalow indifferent.
10	Poshiana . .	8 ,,	Path lies up valley of Sooran river, mostly along its stony bed. Several waterfalls are to be seen. About a mile from village, steep ascent. No bungalow but small mud hut. Tents have to be pitched on the roofs of the houses.
11	Aliabad Serai .	11 ,,	Road easy at first along side of mountain; then crosses river, and enters Nilána valley. At upper end is the Pir Panjál range. Ascent rather hard up zigzag path; top of pass 11,600 feet. Road then gradual slope to the Serai. Grand view from summit of pass. Fair accommodation in the Serai.

The Gújerát and Pir Panjál Route (continued).

No.	Name.	Distance.	Remarks.
	Aliabad Serai to—		
12	Hirpoor . .	12 miles	Road along the valley, at first along side of mountain, and towards end of march opens into the plains of Kashmir. No bungalow, but old Mogul serai.
13	Shupiyan . .	8 „	An easy march along right bank of river. A large town, with good bungalow; supplies abundant.
14	Rámoo . .	11 „	Road easy along the plains; crosses Rembiara river; then ascends hill, and passes through a wood; then descends to Ramchu river. Good bungalow.
15	Srinagar . .	18 „	A long march, but road level all the way, passing through village of Wahtor, from whence road to Srinagar is good, and lined with poplar-trees. On arrival at city cross river; bungalows and encamping-ground will be found on its right bank.

ROUTE NO. 2.

The Ráwal Pindi and Marri Route.

No.	NAME.	DISTANCE.	REMARKS.
	Ráwal Pindi to—		
1	Bárakao . .	13½ miles	The first three stages are usually accomplished in one journey, either by stage-cart or dhooly-dâk. Road good all the way.
2	Tret . . .	12 „	
3	Marri . . .	14½ „	
4	Daywal . .	10 „	Easy march down-hill all the way. Good bungalow, and supplies abundant.
5	Kohála . . .	11 „	Road for first four miles descending to river Jhelam, along the right bank of which the remainder leads. Good dâk. Bungalow close to river.
6	Chatar Kalás .	11½ „	Road crosses river by suspension-bridge, and then skirts it all the way; a fair path, safe to ride. Small but good bungalow.
7	Rára	12 „	Road steep in places; the last part of march it descends to river. Very good bungalow; supplies plentiful.
8	Tináli . . .	12 „	A beautiful march through lovely scenery; road precipitous in places, but rideable nearly all the way. Good bungalow on a level with the river.

The Ráwal Pindi and Marri Route (continued).

No.	Name.	Distance.	Remarks.
	Tinåli to—		
9	Ghari . . .	10 miles	Easy road. Good bungalow.
10	Hatti . . .	12 "	Road very hilly; in several places many hundred feet above the river, and bordering rather ugly precipices. Scenery very fine. A good bungalow.
11	Chakoti . .	15 "	Road broad and good, but very hilly, and with steep precipices in places. Several streams have to be crossed, but all are bridged. Bungalow small, but good.
12	Ooree . . .	16 "	A long march, but over a fair road, which is beautifully shaded throughout, passes over eight deep gorges, and is crossed by several streams, all bridged. A capital bungalow on the top of a plateau surrounded by a high mountain.
13	Oorumboo .	11 "	Road comparatively level; skirts the Jhelam, and is beautifully shady, passing through large forest. Scenery very fine. Good bungalow.

The Ráwal Pindi and Marri Route (continued).

No.	Name.	Distance.	Remarks.
	Oorumboo to—		
14	Báramúla . .	15 miles	Road good; passes through Naoshera, and crosses the Jhelam to town after a pleasant and easy march which conducts one into the Vale itself. At this town, where there is a good double-storied bungalow and abundant supplies, boats can be had, and Srinagar reached in about twenty hours, affording a delightful trip up the river Jhelam and through the Woolar lake.
15	Pattan . . .	14 "	Road very good, and mostly level all the way.
16	Srinagar . .	17 "	Road good, passing at first through fields and the suburbs of Chatterbal; finally down the avenue of poplars near the Palace, and then over the Ameeri Kadal, or first city bridge, to the bungalows and encamping ground set apart for visitors to the capital.

Route No. 3.

The Gújerát and Púnch Route.

This is an alternative route to that over the Pir Panjál Pass, and must be taken when the latter is closed by snow. From Gújerát to Thanna Mundi the route is the same as found on No. 1; and from this place to Ooree, where it joins the Marri route, is six marches, as follows:

No.	Name.	Distance.	Remarks.
	Thanna Mundi to—		
1	Sooran . . .	16 miles	Road passes over Rutten Pir Pass, then into valley of the Sooran river, through which it continues to destination. Fair bungalow.
2	Púnch . . .	14 „	Road continues along valley on right bank of river, the latter end of the march passing through fields. Púnch is a large town, the residence of the Rajah of that State. Good bungalow, and abundant supplies.
3	Kahoota . .	9 „	Road turns to the north, passing up the valley of the Bitarh, a tributary of the Sooran. Bungalow indifferent.
4	Aliabad. . .	8 „	A rough march up a long and narrow valley. Bungalow indifferent.
5	Hydrabad . .	7 „	Short but hard march. The Haji Pir Pass, 8,500 feet high, has to be crossed; path then continues along side of mountain. Bungalow indifferent.

The Gújerát and Púnch Route (continued).

No.	Name.	Distance.	Remarks.
	Hydrabad to—		
6	Ooree . . .	10 miles	Path runs along side of mountain, and is pretty rough at first. A fine waterfall to be seen on the way. Bungalow good.

From Ooree the continuation of the journey is the same as shown on Route No. 2.

Route No. 4.

The Ráwal Pindi and Abbottabad Route.

No.	Name.	Distance.	Remarks.
	Ráwal Pindi to—		
3	Marri . . .	40 miles	Three marches usually performed in one day by stage-cart or dhooly-dâk, as shown on No. 1 Route.
4	Khaira Galli .	9 "	From Marri to Abbottabad the road lies through the mountains, and is a good one, the journey being accomplished in one day by dhooly-dâk or riding—a halt being made, if required, at any of the intermediate stages. Abbottabad is a large station, with a good bungalow and abundant supplies.
5	Doonga Galli .	11 "	
6	Bara Galli . .	8 "	
7	Abbottabad .	14 "	
8	Mánsera . .	13½ "	Easy march over a good road along the plains. Good bungalow.

The Ráwal Pindi and Abbottabad Route (continued).

No.	Name.	Distance.	Remarks.
	Mánsera to—		
9	Ghari . . .	19 miles	A long but easy march—the first half through the plains, the latter half through the mountains; a good road all the way.
10	Mozufferabad.	9 "	Road crosses a range of hills and the Kishenganga river; then ascends to Doobballi pass; then passes along bed of torrent through a narrow gorge which opens into the valley of the Kishenganga. Supplies are abundant, as it is a large town.
11	Hattian . .	17 "	Long, rough march along the right bank of the Jhelam, which is joined by the Kishenganga about a mile from Mozufferabad. Fair bungalow.
12	Kanda . . .	11 "	Easy march. Several ups and downs, as road is very undulating. Fair bungalow.
13	Kathai . . .	12 "	Rough march, very steep in places.
14	Sháhdera . .	12 "	A rough march; several ravines have to be crossed. Good bungalow.
15	Gingle . . .	14 "	An easy march, the road being smooth and level nearly all the way.
16	Báramúla . .	18 "	A long but easy and very pretty march.

Báramúla has been described on Route No. 2, where also will be found the continuation of this road to Srinagar.

APPENDIX II.

TREATY OF AMRITSAR.

Treaty between the British Government on the one part, and MAHARAJAH GOLAB SINGH, *of Jummoo, on the other, concluded on the part of the British Government by* FREDERICK CURRIE, ESQ., *and* BREVET-MAJOR HENRY MONTGOMERY LAWRENCE, *acting under the orders of the* RIGHT HONOURABLE SIR HENRY HARDINGE, G.C.B., *one of Her Britannic Majesty's Honourable Privy Council, Governor-General, appointed by the Honourable Company to direct and control all their affairs in the East Indies, and by* MAHARAJAH GOLAB SINGH *in person.*

ARTICLE 1.—The British Government transfers and makes over for ever, in independent possession to Maharajah Golab Singh, and the heirs male of his body, all the hilly or mountainous country with its dependencies, situated on the eastward of the River Indus and westward of the River Ravee, including Chumba and excluding Lahoul, being part of the territory ceded to the British Government by the Lahore State, according to the provisions of Article 4 of the Treaty of Lahore, dated 9th March, 1846.

ARTICLE 2.—The eastern boundary of the tract, transferred by the foregoing article to Maharajah Golab Singh, shall be laid down by Commissioners appointed by the British Government and Maharajah Golab Singh respectively for that purpose, and shall be defined in a separate engagement after survey.

ARTICLE 3.—In consideration of the transfer made to him and his heirs by the provisions of the foregoing articles, Maharajah Golab Singh will pay to the British Government the sum of seventy-five lacs of rupees (Nánukshåhee), fifty lacs to be paid on ratification of this treaty, and twenty-five lacs on or before the 1st October of the current year, A.D. 1846.

ARTICLE 4.—The limits of the territories of Maharajah Golab Singh shall not be at any time changed without the concurrence of the British Government.

ARTICLE 5.—Maharajah Golab Singh will refer to the arbitration of the British Government any disputes or questions that may arise between himself and the government of Lahore, or any other neighbouring state, and will abide by the decision of the British Government.

ARTICLE 6.—Maharajah Golab Singh engages for himself and heirs to join, with the whole of his military force, the British troops when employed within the hills, or in the territories adjoining his possessions.

ARTICLE 7.—Maharajah Golab Singh engages never to take or retain in his service any British subjects, nor the subjects of any European or American State, without the consent of the British Government.

ARTICLE 8.—Maharajah Golab Singh engages to respect, in regard to the territory transferred to him, the provisions of Articles 5, 6, and 7, of the separate engagement between the British Government and the Lahore Durbar, dated 11th March, 1846.

ARTICLE 9.—The British Government will give its aid to Maharajah Golab Singh in protecting his territories from external enemies.

ARTICLE 10.—Maharajah Golab Singh acknowledges the supremacy of the British Government, and will, in token of such supremacy, present annually to the British Government one horse, twelve perfect shawl-goats, of approved breed (six male and six female), and three pairs of Kashmir shawls.

This treaty, consisting of ten articles, has been this day settled by Frederick Currie, Esq., and Brevet-Major Henry Montgomery Lawrence, acting under the directions of the Right Honourable Sir Henry Hardinge, G.C.B., Governor-General, on the part of the British Government, and by Maharajah Golab Singh in person; and the said treaty has been this day ratified by the seal of the Right Honourable Sir Henry Hardinge, G.C.B., Governor-General.

Done at Amritsar this 16th day of March, in the year of our Lord 1846, corresponding with the 17th day of Rubbee-ool-awul, 1762, Hijree.

APPENDIX III.

Rules for the Guidance of Officers and other Travellers visiting the Dominions of HIS HIGHNESS RUNBEER SINGH, *the Maharajah of Jummoo and Kashmir.*

1. THERE are four authorized routes for European visitors to Kashmir [all of which are noticed in this work]. The special permission of the Punjab Goverment must be obtained by travellers proposing to proceed from Simla to Kashmir across the hills. All other roads are positively forbidden; and in respect to the direct road from Jummoo (the Bunnihal route), the prohibition has been ordered by the Supreme Government at the special request of His Highness the Maharajah. The road branching from Rajaori by Aknoor, which is used by the Maharajah's family and troops, is also expressly prohibited.

2. Every officer or traveller about to visit Kashmir should engage before proceeding a sufficient number of ponies or mules for the conveyance of his baggage.

3. CARRIAGE AND COOLIES.—Coolies employed in carrying baggage, or for other purposes, are to be settled with daily, as in our own provinces, and their loads should not exceed twenty-five seers. Taboos, or mules, should not carry more than two maunds in the hills.

4. It is necessary to bear in mind that coolies and carriages are not available on the spot, but they have usually to be collected from distant villages. Travellers on reaching a stage should

therefore send forward to the next a notice of their requisitions, and must not expect to be supplied at a moment's warning. This intimation is especially necessary in the case of officers hurrying back to save their leave, and sometimes making double stages. In this case double hire must invariably be paid.

5. In returning from Kashmir, coolies or carriages should not be taken on beyond the Maharajah's frontier, as it causes much inconvenience to other travellers.

6. ENCAMPING-PLACES AND SUPPLIES.—Officers should encamp at the fixed stages and encamping-grounds, otherwise supplies may not be forthcoming. They should avoid entering or pitching inside villages, where quarrels may occur between their servants and the public of the country.

7. All arrangements for supplies, coolies, or baggage animals, and all references to the local authorities, should be made through the proper attendants; but payment for supplies, coolies, and carriage should be made by travellers themselves in their presence.

8. No interference is to be offered to Kardars (revenue officers), Thanadars, or Kotwals (police officers), or other servants or subjects of His Highness the Maharajah; and no calls are to be made on them except in real emergencies. All payments are to be made at the rates demanded, which, if exorbitant, can be afterwards reported to the officer on duty at Srinagar.

9. A book will be presented at each stage, in which every traveller is required to write legibly his name, rank, station, and the date of his arrival.

10. SHOOTING EXCURSIONS.—When going out on shooting excursions visitors are to take carriage and supplies with them, and not to persist in demanding them at places where they are not procurable. They are not to press into their service the people of the country as beaters for game.

11. References in Cases of Difficulties or Disputes.—In any case of dispute officers should avoid putting themselves in direct collision with the authorities, soldiers, servants, or subjects of the Maharajah. They are also warned not to place entire confidence in the statements of their servants, who have often their own objects to serve.

12. Should they have reason to consider that they or their followers have been ill-treated or affronted, they are strictly prohibited from taking the law into their own hands, or punishing the offending parties; but they are to make known their complaint to the authorities on the spot, and immediately to report the matter to the officer on deputation at Srinagar.

13. All such cases which may occur at the capital are to be preferred at once to the officer on deputation, who is there for the purpose of maintaining order. Officers are not themselves to repair to the durbar of the Maharajah, or the courts of his delegates, or to communicate directly with them.

14. Observance of Local Laws and Customs.—Officers are enjoined to remember that they are visitors in the remote dominions of an independent sovereign, where they one and all represent the character of their country. If on any occasion they or their servants be brought in contact with the Maharajah, his sons, relatives, or any of his agents, they must treat them with respect and courtesy, and be guided by and conform to the local laws and usages.

15. Officers are not allowed to take away with them, either in their service or with their camps, any subjects of the Maharajah without obtaining permission and a passport from the authorities.

16. They are strictly required to settle all accounts before they quit Kashmir, and to be responsible that the debts of their servants are similarly discharged.

17. All Presents to be Refused.—Presents of every description must be rigidly refused. To take any 'russud' or supplies without payment is positively prohibited, except on the first or last days of a visitor's stay at Kashmir, when it may happen that 'russud' is sent expressly by the Maharajah.

18. Instances having been brought to notice of European visitors to Kashmir having permitted the goods of native merchants to be mixed up with their own, with the object of evading the customs' duties leviable thereupon by the Kashmir Government,—it is hereby pointed out that such conduct will involve legal penalties; and in the case of persons in the civil or military service of the Queen will be reported to the Supreme Government.

19. The Maharajah occasionally invites European visitors to entertainments, at which, if the invitation be accepted, they should appear in undress uniform or evening costume.

20. It will be the duty of the officer on special duty to report to the Punjab Government any officer or traveller infringing any of these rules.

21. Should any officer be guilty of any aggravated breach of decorum or propriety, or of violating the local laws and usages of the country, or other grave misconduct, the civil officer on special duty at Srinagar is empowered to call upon such officer to quit forthwith the territories of the Maharajah. Such requisition on the part of the civil officer must be promptly complied with. An appeal from the order of expulsion will lie, in the case of a first offence, to a court of three experienced officers, whom the civil officer is empowered to summon for hearing such appeals, and the decision of these officers will be final. In the case of a second offence, there will be no appeal against the order of the civil officer.

T. H. Thornton,
Secretary to Government, Punjab.

APPENDIX IV.

Local Rules for the guidance of Visitors in Kashmir, published under the sanction of the Punjab Government.

1. VISITORS wishing to visit the Fort and Palace are required to give notice of their intention on the previous day to the Bábú deputed to attend on European visitors.

2. Visitors about to proceed into the interior, and wishing to be supplied with carriage, are requested to communicate with the Bábú at least thirty hours before the time fixed for their departure. Failing this notice, the Bábú cannot be responsible for the supply of carriage in proper time.

3. Cows and bullocks are under no circumstances to be slain in the territories of His Highness the Maharajah.

4. Visitors are not permitted to take up their abode in the town, in the Dilawar Khan Bágh, or in the gardens on the Dal Lake; viz., the Nishát and the Shalimar Gardens, and the Chashma Sháhi. The Nasim Bágh is available for camping. The fixed camping-places in Srinagar are as follows: the Ram Munshi, Munshi, Hari Singh, and Chenar Bághs.

5. Servants of visitors found in the city after dark, and any servant found without a light after the evening gun has fired, will be liable to be apprehended by the police.

6. Servants of visitors resorting to other places than the fixed latrines will be liable to punishment.

7. Grass-cutters are prohibited from cutting grass in, or in the neighbourhood of, the gardens occupied by European visitors.

8. All boats are to be moored on the left bank of the river, and no boatmen are allowed to remain at night on the right bank.

9. When the Dal gate is closed no attempt should be made to remove the barrier, or to lift boats over the bund to or from the lake.

10. Visitors are not permitted to shoot in the tract of country extending along the lake from the Takt-i-Suliman to the Shálimár gardens, which is a preserve of His Highness the Maharajah; shooting on the tracts marginally noted, which are private property, is also prohibited.

Doputta
Kukaiwalla
Machípura
Danna Chikar
Oori
Bunyár

11. Visitors are prohibited from shooting the heron in Kashmir.

12. Fishing is prohibited at the places marginally noted, as also between the first and third bridges in Srinagar.

Martand, Vernàg, Anat Nág, Devi, Khírpowáni

13. Houses have been built by His Highness the Maharajah for the accommodation of visitors—those in the Munshi Bágh being set aside for the use of married people, and those in the Hari Singh Bágh for bachelors. With the exception of the houses reserved by His Highness for his private guests, and those reserved for the Civil Surgeon, dispensary, and library, all the houses are available for visitors, and are allotted by the Bábú.

14. Married visitors are allowed to leave the houses occupied by them for a term of seven days without being required permanently to vacate the same. After the expiration of that period, the Bábú is empowered to make over the premises to another visitor requiring house accommodation; any property left by the

former occupant being liable to removal at the owner's risk. Bachelors are allowed to leave their houses for a period of three days subject to the same conditions.

15. Visitors are required to conform strictly with all local laws and usages.

16. In all matters when they may require redress, and especially on the occurrence of robberies, visitors are informed that they should refer as soon as practicable to the officer on Special Duty.

17. Visitors are particularly requested to be careful that their servants do not import into, or export from, the Valley articles for sale on which duty is liable. The baggage of visitors is not examined by the Maharajah's Customs officials, and in return for this courtesy it is expected that any evasion of the Customs Regulations will be discountenanced.

W HENDERSON,
Officer on Special Duty, Kashmir.

APPENDIX V.

TARIFF OF BOAT HIRE.

THE hire of a doongah, with crew, is fifteen Government rupees per mensem. The crew should consist of at least four persons; womcn, and children over twelve years of age, to be considered as able-bodied members of a crew.

The hire of a shikárá is determined by the number of the crew, who are paid at the rate of three Government rupees per mensem, and eight annas for the boat. When boats are taken out of Srinagar, boatmen are entitled to rassad at the rate of half an anna per man per diem.

TARIFF OF DOONGAH-HIRE BY DISTANCE.

		r.	a.	p.
From Baramula to Srinagar, per boatman	. .	0	8	0
" Srinagar to Búramúla	" . .	0	6	0
" Srinagar to Islámábád	" . .	0	8	0
" Islámábád to Srinagar	" . .	0	6	0
" Srinagar to Awantipur	" . .	0	6	0
" Srinagar to Manasbal, for the trip	. .	1	0	0
" Srinagar to Gánderbal	" . .	1	2	0
" Srinagar to Awatkula	" . .	3	0	0

When boats are ordered from Srinagar to meet a visitor at any place, half hire of the boat from Srinagar is payable in addition to the fare to the place whence the visitor is proceeding. When a boat is not used on the date for which it is ordered, eight annas per diem are payable for detention.

W. HENDERSON,
Officer on Special Duty, Kashmir.

APPENDIX VI.

KASHMIR POSTAL RULES.

PUNJAB GAZETTE, NO. 673, GENERAL DEPARTMENT, 16TH MARCH, 1867.

The following arrangements for Postal communication with Kashmir during the ensuing season, have been made in communication with the Kashmir Government and the Postmaster-General of the Punjab.

1. ALL letters for Srinagar and the Valley of Kashmir will be forwarded *viâ* Marri.

2. At Marri the letters will be placed in a sealed bag, and made over to an official of the Maharajah of Kashmir, who will convey the bag to the civil officer on duty at Srinagar.

3. The bag will be opened, and the letters sorted, by an official attached to the office of the civil officer.

4. All letters for visitors at Srinagar and their followers will be distributed through the agency placed at the disposal of the civil officer. Other letters will be made over to the diwan of the Maharajah at Srinagar for distribution.

5. In addition to the English postage, a fee, equal to half the English postage, will be levied on all letters delivered at Srinagar.

6. A post-office will be opened at or near the residence of the civil officer, for the convenience of visitors to Kashmir and their

U 2

followers; and letters for British territory will be despatched in a sealed bag to Marri, and made over to the postal authorities at that place.

7. All covers intended for despatch from Srinagar to British territory by the above dâk, which for convenience will be designated the resident's dâk, should be marked 'per resident's dâk,' in English, and signed at the lower left-hand corner by the sender; they must further bear, in addition to the English postage, a Kashmir postage-stamp, of half the value of the English stamp required, otherwise they will be made over to the diwan to be returned to the sender, if known, or otherwise disposed of according to the rules of the Kashmir post-office.—By order,

T. H. THORNTON,
Secretary to Government, Punjab.

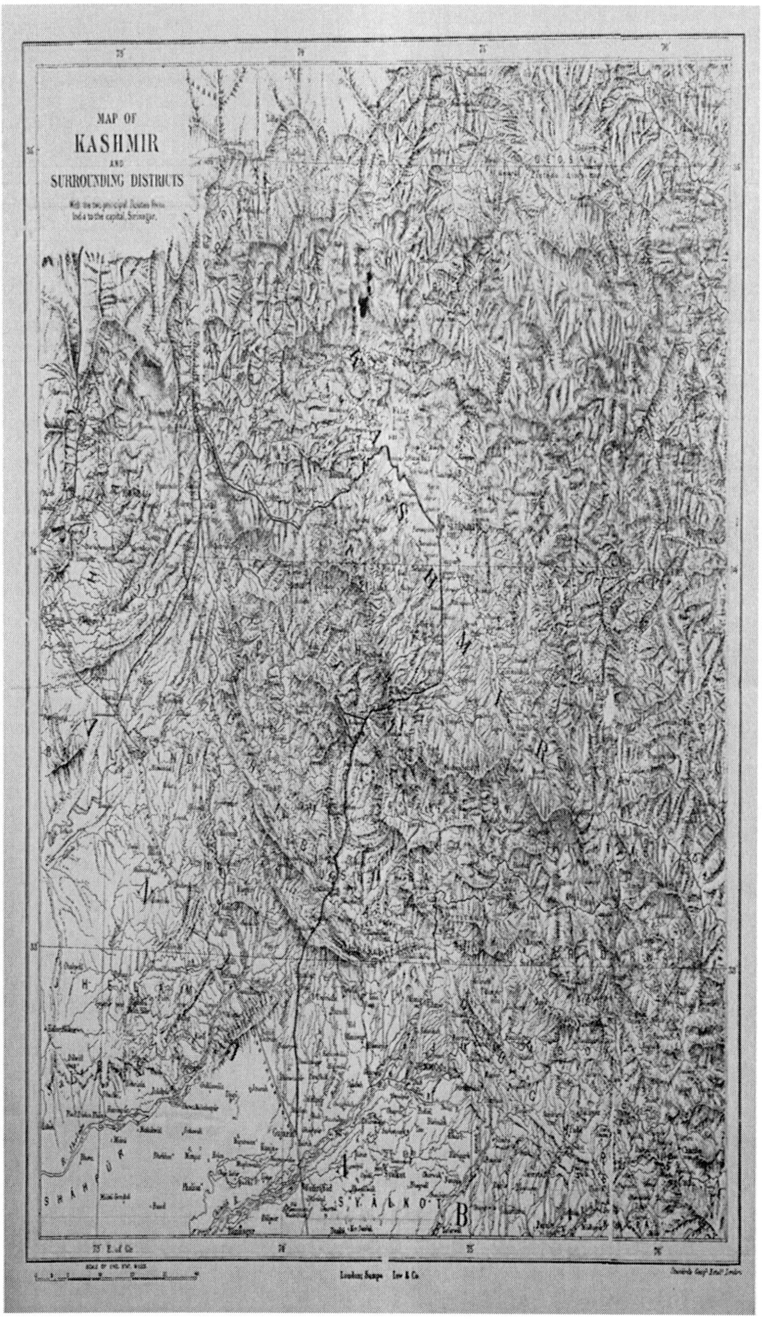
MAP OF
KASHMIR
AND
SURROUNDING DISTRICTS
KASHMIR
SYALKOT

INDEX.